THE SCRIPTURE GUIDE

A FAMILIAR INTRODUCTION
TO THE STUDY OF THE BIBLE

JAMES W. ALEXANDER

SOLID GROUND CHRISTIAN BOOKS
BIRMINGHAM, ALABAMA USA

SOLID GROUND CHRISTIAN BOOKS
PO Box 660132, Vestavia Hills, AL 35266
205-443-0311
sgcb@charter.net
http://www.solid-ground-books.com

THE SCRIPTURE GUIDE
A Familiar Introduction to the Study of the Bible

by James Waddel Alexander (1804-1859)

First published in 1838 by The American Sunday School Union, Philadelphia, PA

Published by Solid Ground Christian Books

Classic Reprints Series

First printing December 2004

ISBN: 1-932474-64-1

Manufactured in the United States of America

Uncovering Another Buried Treasure

The Scripture Guide by James Waddel Alexander is the latest 'buried treasure' that Solid Ground Christian Books has been enabled to uncover. Written over 150 years ago, it is a priceless gem intended to awaken a desire to begin a lifelong study of the Sacred Scriptures.

J.W. Alexander was the first born son of Archibald Alexander of Princeton Seminary fame. In the words of John Hall, one of James' dearest friends, "His mind labored with schemes for the diffusion of healthful and conservative influences throughout all classes of society. The threatenings of infidelity and social disorganization aroused his anxious efforts to interpose the Bible and Christianity as the only effectual antidote. His main hopes rested in the making of Holy Scripture the great organ of mental and spiritual development in education. And this, as usual with him, was a practical opinion. He was all the time working in that field: writing for children, for young men, for Sunday-school; and his publications of every sort will be found marked with that strong impress of his theory, itself derived from revelation, that draughts, pure, direct, and constant, from the fountain of inspired truth, are the most salutary and only sufficient remedy for the evils of the times. To this great result were the incessant productions of his pen addressed, from the series of miniature toy-books for infants, and the Sunday School 'The Scripture Guide: an Introduction to the Scriptures,' [here reprinted] to such profound dissertations as the paper on 'Transcendentalism,' in the *Biblical Repertory,* the joint production of himself and the late Professor Dod, the force and ability of which made it celebrated as an Evangelical weapon, as well as an exploit in the field of metaphysics" (quote taken from *Mourning a Fallen Shepherd* to be published in 2005 by SGCB).

This volume deserves a place in every home where God is loved and the Bible is honored. It was written in the form of a story so that it would gain and maintain the attention of even the younger readers. It is written with a depth of wisdom that will instruct teachers and students alike. Of all the 'buried treasure' we have uncovered, by the mercy of the Lord, this may well head the list. Take up and read it, and share what you have learned.

The Publisher
Thanksgiving 2004

PREFACE.

THE great end of all religious teaching would be attained, if men could be brought to read the Bible aright. No books, therefore, are unimportant, which point to the Holy Scriptures. Such is the present attempt, which is expressly dedicated to the YOUNG. It is intended for excitement as well as instruction ; not only to communicate information and explain difficulties, but to offer inducements for the study of the Bible.

When a copy of our English Bible is placed in the hand of an inquiring, but uninstructed young person, there naturally arise a number of interesting questions. Is this the work of one, or of many hands? Is it an original work, or a version? At what times and in what tongue was it written? Into what languages has it been translated? What is the history of our common version? How am I to interpret the division into books, chapters, and verses; the numerous marginal notes; and the peculiarities of typography? How may it be studied to the best advantage?—These are inquiries which even children of inquisitive minds are prompt to make; and which even intelligent teachers are sometimes at a loss to satisfy. It is such questions that the following work professes to answer.

There are numerous works on these subjects addressed to the learned; but they are beyond the reach of common readers. There are also many treatises which direct to the proper study of the sacred text. But it is believed, that there is not in our language any book which presents at one view exactly the field which is here exhibited. In justification of this remark, the reader is requested to examine the contents of the chapters from the sixth to the eleventh, inclusively.

The form of the work may seem to demand some explanation. It is by no means a fictitious composition, or a mere book of amusement. Yet, as some of the matters treated, however important, are in themselves somewhat dry, the author has spared no pains to render it attractive and even entertaining.

The dialogue offered an occasion for constant change of subject, and for the suggestion of many questions, which, in any other method of composition, would have been an interruption to the discourse.

The subject is by no means exhausted. Among the important topics which could not be fully treated within our narrow limits, are such as the following : An analysis of each book of Scripture ; a key to Scripture difficulties, and especially to the prophetical writings ; a catalogue of such books as are useful aids to the Bible student ; and a history of the distribution of the Scriptures by Bible Societies. These may be treated in a subsequent volume.

It is the earnest desire and prayer of the author, that these pages may be made the means of promoting the interests of true religion, by inducing some, at least, to read the best of books with increased profit and delight.

CONTENTS.

AN

INTRODUCTION

TO

THE SCRIPTURES.

CHAPTER I.

Introduction—Account of uncle Austin—The holidays—Visit to Oakdale—Meeting with uncle Austin—Conversation with him—Walk over the grounds.

ERNEST and Hilary were the sons of Mr. Miller of New York. They were sensible boys, and had been taught in the best schools of the city. Ernest was the elder; but his brother had so much sprightliness, that they were almost always learning the same things; and they looked very much alike, so that people sometimes took them for twins.

When the winter came on, and they had been going very steadily to school, they began to think of getting free from their books. They were sitting by a bright coal-fire in the little back-room, one evening in December, when Hilary shut up his grammar, and said, " Ernest, it is time to think about Christmas; where are we going to spend the holidays?"

"I heard father say," said Ernest, "that we are to go and see uncle Austin, in New Jersey; and I am very glad of it, for I like uncle Austin. You were never at his house—were you, Hilary?"

"No, brother; you remember I had broken my collar-bone, and could not go out, when you went to Jersey. Tell me something about him. What is he like?"

"Like!" said Ernest; "why, he is like one of the best men in the world. He is like one of the good old folks we read about in the Bible. He has gray hair hanging down over his neck, and when he goes out he walks with a cane. But he is so kind and so gentle! I never heard a cross word out of his mouth. When Tom and I broke his great inkstand, and blacked all his papers, he only said, 'O, children, children; I shall have to teach you the way to be careful!'"

"O, then, I am sure," said Hilary, "he will give us a Christmas present!"

"Do not be thinking about Christmas presents, Hilary. Uncle Austin will do better than that. He will give us such good talk, and tell us so many pretty histories, and show us so many curiosities, and draw us so many pictures, that you will forget all about Christmas boxes, and the like."

Hilary looked sober for a while, and then said: "Brother Ernest, is this the same uncle that the boys used to call the *Bible man?*"

"Yes," said Ernest, "this is he. Whenever he went out walking, he used to carry Bibles and New Testaments in his great old-fashioned pockets, to give away to the poor people. This made them call him the *Bible man.* But besides this, you know he used to be a great traveller; and when he came from sea, some years ago, he brought with him several boxes of books. When the boxes were opened, they were full of Bibles!"

Hilary. Why what could he do with so many?

Ernest. I will tell you. There is a society in England called the British and Foreign Bible Society. They get Bibles in all languages, and send them all over the world. When uncle Austin was in London, he says that he was so delighted to see the great piles of Bibles for the heathen people, that the tears ran down his face. He bought one Bible in each of the languages, and brought them over to America with him. They fill several shelves in his library.

Hilary. Can he read in them all?

Ernest. O, no! He can read in a number of them, because he has lived in a great many different countries. But then, he says it is a memorial of the Bible Society. Whenever he looks at his shelves of Bibles, he thinks of the good men who are trying to send the Bible all over the earth. He has given away a number of them to poor Frenchmen, and Spaniards, and others. And when there was a Greek in his neighbourhood, he sent him a present of a New Testament in modern Greek.

Hilary. Uncle Austin must be a great scholar.

Ernest. He is a great Bible scholar. He reads in the Bible more than in all his other books. And this is another reason why the neighbours call him the *Bible man.* Whenever they come in, they find him at his Bible.

Hilary. I wonder he does not get tired of reading so much in one book. *I* get tired of reading a single hour in the Bible.

Ernest. And you ought to be ashamed of it. But only go to uncle Austin's, and he will explain it all to you. I cannot say the things as he says them ; but I can tell you this, that ever since I was at *Oakdale*, where he lives, I have had very different thoughts about the Bible.

Hilary. Well, it may be so : but I hope he has somebody to cook the Christmas dinner, and make the pies and cakes, while he is at his books.

Ernest. There you are at your jokes again! Why, Hilary, you would make one think that you care for nothing but eating. Uncle Austin is a widower. His wife has been dead more than twenty years. But he has a good kind niece, who is our cousin, who takes good care of the house-keeping. And the old gardener, John, will be sure to be attentive to the "little masters," as he calls the boys.

The boys then turned to their books, and studied as usual until the family were called to family worship. When they retired to bed, Hilary thought a great deal about the approaching holidays. In the morning, he awaked his brother, and said, "Ernest, are you sure that this good old uncle of our's will be glad to see us?"

"Yes," said Ernest, "his face will be bright with joy."

"But," said Hilary, "if he studies the Bible so much, and is so very religious, I should think he would be very solemn and dry."

"That," replied Ernest, "is one of your ignorant notions. When you see uncle Austin, you will see that religion does not make people gloomy. He is a happy old gentleman, and he loves the little children so much, that he often carries bundles of little books to give away at the doors of the country schools. But I will tell you one thing; you had better be brushing up your knowledge of the Bible before you go, for uncle sometimes asks some hard questions."

The holidays came at last. The boys were up

before daylight, in order to get ready. Their trunks were packed, and their great-coats spread out. The young travellers could scarcely be content to wait for the carriage. At length it came to the door; there was much shaking of hands, and abundance of messages and good wishes, and then the carriage drove off. The ground was covered with a light snow, and the sleet of the preceding night had settled in a glassy coat upon the trees and shrubs. When the sun shone out, the whole country glistened, as if every icicle had been a crystal or a precious stone.

The journey need not be described. It was like most journeys in which boys are concerned. Ernest was stretching his neck one way, and Hilary was stretching his neck another way, both eager to see every thing, and both delighted at every thing they saw. Hilary talked most and laughed most; but Ernest looked wise, as if he were ashamed to admire any thing too much. They were glad when they found they were drawing near to Oakdale.

"There! there it is!" cried Ernest. "Look out, Hilary! Look out! There is uncle's barn; there is the little brook, and the bridge over it; there is the row of oaks; and now I see the house; and the green cedars before the door! And, O! there is good uncle Austin himself, with his blue cloak on, waiting for us, and his staff in his hand."

The carriage stopped. The step was let down. The door was opened; Ernest stepped out. The good old man cried, "Welcome, welcome, nephew!" and, taking Ernest in his arms, he kissed his forehead. "And this is my nephew Hilary? I must take you in my old arms too. But come in, Hilary—come in, Ernest—the day is cold—the parlour is all warm for you, and every one glad to see you, even down to Hylax the dog."

Old John, the gardener, took in the luggage; and uncle Austin led the way into the house. Miss Priscilla More, his niece, was standing there to receive her cousins. They found a bright country fire, roaring in a large old-fashioned hearth. A high arm-chair was before it. In this the old gentleman seated himself, and then pointed to a low chair on his right, and another on his left: "There are your seats, my lads," said he, cheerfully; "Ernest, sit on my right; Hilary, sit on my left: now be as happy as you can."

By the time the boys had got well warmed, and somewhat rested, they were called into the next room to dinner. The young travellers sat down with good appetites, and I must confess that Hilary thought more highly of Oakdale than he had ever done, when he saw the bountiful provision which had been made by his cousin Priscilla. During the meal, uncle Austin looked very attentively at his nephews, and smiled with pleasure when he saw how well they behaved themselves. After dinner, they returned to the warm parlour, and drew their chairs again around the fire. Uncle Austin leaned back in his chair, and began as follows :

" I have been thinking how rapidly time flies. It seems but a little while since I used to go to my grandfather's, to spend my winter holidays. And now I am old enough to be your grandfather."

Hilary said, " Uncle Austin, how old would your grandfather be, if he were living now ?"

" O, my child, he would be the oldest man on earth ; for he was very old then, and it was sixty years ago ; he would be a hundred and fifty years old."

" That is not as old by twenty-five years as Abraham was," said Ernest.

" I am glad you know so much about Abraham, nephew. Men lived to be older in those days. Pray, master Hilary, how old was Enoch when he died ?"

Hilary smiled, and said, " Just as old, sir, as Elijah was."

" Well done !" said uncle Austin. " I thought I had caught you : but you have looked a little into the best of books. It is well that you do. As for me, I began too late. When I was of your age, there was no such thing as a Sunday-school, and very few books to explain the Bible. When we wanted to read, we used to get little gilt books from Mr. Newberry, of St. Paul's Churchyard, London. We had Jack the Giant-killer, Guy of Warwick, and the Seven Sleepers. But I cared little for reading of any kind. My delight was to ride, and shout, and frolic. And when I began to read the Bible some years after, it was quite a strange book to me."

Ernest. Uncle, how old were you when you went to France?

Uncle. I have been several times to France, my boy. The first time I was twenty-three years old, and then I travelled all over Europe; but the time I stayed longest in France was when I was about forty years of age. And now I am content to remain here, and lay my bones in America.

Hilary. But, uncle, we never see you in the city. You must get very tired of staying always here in this lonely place.

Uncle. Not at all, Hilary. There you make a boyish mistake. I dare say you think that nobody can be happy unless he lives in New York, and walks in Broadway, and sees abundance of fine stores, and fine people, and fine ships. You fancy that I am lonesome. Now let me tell you, I am happier here in my quiet Oakdale, than many a man who lives in a marble house, among thousands of gay citizens.

Hilary But what can you do with yourself? Whom have you got to talk with?

Here uncle Austin looked very archly at the little boy, and said, as he rose from his chair, " Do you see that mahogany door? I have a number of friends within, with whom I talk every day."

Hilary. Ah, uncle! you think to catch me again You mean your *books*. Now, do you not, uncle?

Uncle. I do, indeed. Is it not a strange thing that I cannot entrap such a little fellow as you are? I suppose I shall have to show you my library. But we will first take a walk, and while we walk I will tell you something about my place.

Hilary ran to get his uncle's cane, Ernest brought his coat, and Miss Priscilla tied a handkerchief around his neck. Then taking his hat, the good old man gave an arm to each of the boys, and led them out to survey the farm and grounds.

" Yonder," said he, " is the place where your dear mother was born. The old house used to stand between those large oaks. It was burned down twenty years ago. And there is a ruinous house, which, in old times, was a distillery; but we have learned to do without distilleries, and the house is now used for a tool-house by the gardener. There is a hedge which I have amused myself in making. There is a row of pear trees which I planted when I was a boy. There is a broken tree which I saw struck with lightning many years ago. And on the other side of the bridge is a little row of houses, which I have built for some of my poor neighbours. In the opposite direction, you may see the steeple of the church rising among the trees. Thus you see, my dear children, that whenever I come out of my doors, I see something or other to remind me of past days."

The boys now began to roam over the farm, and the old gentleman, finding it cold, returned to the house. Here he had a fire made in his library, and prepared several things for the amusement of his nephews, whom he loved very much.

CHAPTER II.

Uncle Austin's study—Hebrew map—The Bible the most en
tertaining book in the world—Histories in the Bible—Bible
histories are all true—Greatly neglected—It is God's book
Inspiration explained—The Bible tells us of Christ—The
Gospels.

WHEN it began to grow dark, Ernest and Hilary
returned to the house, and were immediately conducted to their uncle's study. Hilary had now an
opportunity to see for himself what his brother
had told him. *The study*, as it was always called,
was a large room in the pleasantest part of the
house. A row of windows on the eastern side
made it very light and cheerful, and the opposite
wall was entirely covered with handsome shelves,
full of books. Between the windows were several
paintings and maps, and over the chimney-piece
was a plan of the city of Jerusalem. Hilary had
never seen such a place before. He was used to
his father's store and counting-room, and you could
hardly have shown him any thing new in the way
of merchandise; but he was not so much acquainted
with books. After he had gazed about him for a
time, his uncle said to him, " Come here, nephew,
and sit near the lamp, for I have something to show

you. What is this, Hilary, which I hold in my hand ?"

Hilary. It looks like a pocket handkerchief, sir.

Ernest. It looks more like a map.

Hilary. But who ever saw a map on a piece of red cotton cloth ?

Ernest. Who ever saw a handkerchief with mountains, and lakes, and rivers on it ? Yes, and here I see the latitude and longitude.

Uncle. You are both right. It is a handkerchief with a map painted on it. The map represents the Holy Land. The names are in Hebrew. It is so printed (or rather lithographed) for the convenience of Jews travelling to Palestine. The map is a very correct one ; I obtained it from Trieste, where it was made.*

Ernest. Would not that map help one to understand the Bible ?

Uncle. It would help one who could read Hebrew : but we have better maps of Palestine. There, over the sofa, hangs an excellent map published by the American Sunday-school Union.

Hilary. Why do you think so much of the Bible, uncle ? Almost all your books and pictures have something to do with the Bible.

Uncle. A very proper question. I have found

---

* Such a map is in the author's possession.

out that I have more entertainment from this book than from any thing else.

Ernest. Entertainment! Why, uncle, I never thought of getting entertainment from the Bible. I thought it was the most serious book in the world.

Uncle. So it is, but also entertaining. There is such a thing as *serious* entertainment. It is the best sort. One does not become weary of it so soon. I love to read about the people of ancient times—their greatness, their adventures, and their wonderful deeds. I have other reasons for liking this holy book, which I mean to give you at another time. But, as you are boys, and not old men, I mentioned the entertainment it affords.

Ernest. But, uncle Austin, I do not understand you. When I want to be entertained, I like to read in histories about battles, and generals, and such things. I like to read about the adventures of Captain Cook, and Baron Trenck; or about Alexander the Great, and Hannibal, and Peter of Russia. And I read in the Bible to learn what is good.

Uncle. True, the Bible teaches us concerning God, and our duty; but God has been so condescending as to make it at the same time the most interesting book in the world. If you like to read of adventures, this book is full of them; and what is more, they are all true. There is not a word from beginning to end which is not true. Ernest likes to read of great captains and wars. I am afraid he has something of the soldier in him. Now the Bible has the most remarkable accounts of this kind. There never was a greater commander than *Moses*.

Ernest. Moses! Uncle, are you in earnest?

Uncle. To be sure I am in earnest. Moses was a great general. Just think of what he did. He led out more than a million of people through a sea, and through a desert, and through the land of enemies, to the border of Canaan. And he was forty years their leader. What other general ever did this? And he wrote the account of it himself, and here we have it all in the Bible.

Ernest. Cæsar also wrote about his own wars.

Uncle. Yes; I am glad you take notice of this. Listen again. *Joshua* was a great captain. *Jephthah* was a remarkable commander. *Samson* was a hero, greater than Hercules. His history is wonderful. If we had never heard of it before, and some one should tell us about him, we should think it more interesting than any of our story-books. *David* was a noble general; he was brave and generous; and his life is as pleasant to read as a novel. And then *Ezra* and *Nehemiah* were two fearless, independent men, who loved their country, and delivered their city from being a ruin.

Hilary. I never thought of this before. But, uncle, I am not like Ernest; I do not care half so much about fighting, and armies, as he does. When I read in Cæsar about his wars, I am wearied out. I am fond of adventures. I like the Arabian Nights, and Gulliver's Travels, and Robinson Crusoe; but mother takes them away from me, because they are untrue.

Uncle. Very right. Some children would read nothing else, if they were not checked. But take the Bible, and study it well, and you will read abundance of adventures and wonders too. But take notice of this—*they are all true.* God himself assures us that they are all true.

Hilary. Perhaps I have skipped them when I have read in the Bible.

Uncle. No. I understand how it is. I also used to consider it a dull and tedious book; but the more I read in it, the more interesting it grows. You can hardly open it without finding some wonderful narrative. The history of our blessed Lord and Saviour Jesus Christ is exceedingly wonderful and affecting too. His birth at Bethlehem—his miracles—his feeding thousands—his stilling the tempest—his raising the girl, and the widow's son, and Lazarus—all are most delightful histories. And then what did you ever read so wonderful as his trial, his crucifixion, his resurrection, his ascension, his appearing to Stephen, and to Saul, and to John?

Hilary. Are there such wonderful things in the first part of the Bible?

Uncle. Surely there are. Have you never read of Daniel in the lion's den—of Elijah and Enoch, who were carried to heaven without ever dying—of the army of Gideon—of the sun and moon standing still—of the manna—of the pillar of cloud—of the flood—of the tower of Babel? Then of all the histories I ever read, I never saw any one so interesting and affecting as that of Joseph. It is hard to read it without weeping.

Hilary. I wonder then that people do not read the Bible more.

Uncle. So do I. It is strange to see how ignorant many in this Christian land are about this sacred book. Some who pass for educated men and women are as ignorant as the rest. They cannot tell how many books are in the Bible, though they pretend to read in it every day. They cannot tell who wrote it, or when it was written, or how many languages it was written in. They do not know where the places are that are mentioned in Scripture. And while they are so ignorant, they cannot take any interest in the book. It is like a box of jewels in a man's house, which he never opens.

Ernest. Uncle, I wish you would tell us some of these things, for I am one of these ignorant people. I know the Bible is a box of precious jewels; but I cannot open it.

Uncle. I must try to give you a key. And it will be a great pleasure to me to show you and Hilary how you may enjoy this treasure.

Hilary. O do so, dear uncle; for I begin to see that I have never thought enough of this book.

Uncle. You must not expect me to tell you all I have to say in a single day, or even a single week. We will converse about this matter every day, and a little at a time. Then you will not be weary. There is one great reason why we should prize the Bible above all other books. I suppose you can guess what I mean.

Ernest. It is God's book.

Uncle. That is the very thing I meant. It is God's own book. It is the only book which was written by inspiration.

Hilary. What is *inspiration?*

Uncle. I mean that the good men who wrote the Scriptures did not themselves find out the things which they wrote. They did not make up the Scriptures by their own wisdom. They wrote down what God told them. God put the things into their minds, and kept them from making mis-takes. That is, God *inspired* them. This teaching is called *inspiration.* " Holy men of God spake as they were moved (inspired) of the Holy Ghost." 2 Pet. i. 21.

Ernest. Then we are sure every word in the Scriptures is true.

Uncle. Yes ; every word ; just as true as if God were to speak it to us from heaven.

Hilary. Is this the reason why the Bible is sometimes called the *Word of God?*

Uncle. It is so. It is the message of God to men.

Hilary. But some of the things in the Bible are spoken by wicked people, like Judas Iscariot, and even by Satan.

Uncle. Very true. God gives us the *account* of what is thus said by the wicked. And God's *account* of what they said is true, even if the words of the wicked men or the devil are not true. If you were to hear, that on a certain day God would speak out of heaven, and tell you what his will is ; would you not be very serious ? Would you not be anxious to hear what might be said ? Would you not believe every word ?

Ernest and Hilary. O, yes !

Uncle. If God, instead of speaking out of heaven, were to write down his holy law with his own hand, would you not think it very precious ? Would you not read it again and again ?

Both. Yes.

Uncle. But God *did* write the commandments in this very way, and he gave them to Moses; and we have a copy of them, made by Moses, in the twentieth chapter of Exodus.

Hilary. O! I never considered that. It is so indeed.

Uncle. But suppose, instead of writing with his own hand, God should instruct a holy man, and inspire him to write down his own will on paper. And suppose this paper should be put into your hands. What should you think of it?

Ernest. I think I should read it till I knew all that was in it.

Uncle. This is just what God has actually done. He instructed the prophets and apostles by his Holy Spirit. He inspired them to tell us his truth and his will. He kept them from all mistakes. And they wrote down the words of God. And the book containing what they wrote is put into our hands. And this book is the *Bible.*

Hilary. Then the Bible is a great deal better than all other books.

Uncle. Indeed it is. It gives us an account of things which no mortal could ever have found out, unless God had inspired him. And it teaches us about the Son of God, and what he said and did when he was upon earth.

Hilary. What an honour it was to hear Christ talk !

Ernest. Uncle, I often think I should have loved to see Christ, and to hear him teaching.

Uncle. Suppose you knew a man who had heard Jesus preach; would you not desire him to tell you what our Saviour said ?

Ernest. Yes ; I think I would travel a great way to see such a man.

Uncle. But suppose this man should save you the trouble of travelling to see him, and should write you a letter. And suppose he should put down in this letter a great many things that Christ said.

Hilary. Why, uncle Austin, such a letter would be worth a thousand dollars.

Uncle. Boys, take notice—there were a number of men who heard Christ preach.

Ernest. O, yes—the apostles ; but they are dead.

Uncle. The apostles heard the blessed Saviour, and learned the truth from his own lips. They are dead, I know. But some of them did exactly what I imagined. They have written to us. And they have put down in their writing a great many things that Christ said.

Hilary. I understand you, uncle. You mean the gospels.

Uncle. Matthew and *John* were apostles ; they wrote down what the blessed Saviour said, and what he did, and here we have it all in the New Testament. *Mark* and *Luke* were pious men, who were always with the apostles, and who were inspired to write the same. Read what Luke says about his knowledge of Christ. Luke i. 2—4. *James,* and *Peter,* and *Jude* were apostles who also wrote. And *Paul* was inspired to write more than all the rest. So you see the Bible is a great and lovely book.

Just then Miss Priscilla opened the door to say that tea was ready.

CHAPTER III.

Egypt—The Bible gives us the earliest account of Egypt—It
is the oldest book in the world—Our only history of early
times—The book of greatest wisdom—Folly of heathens and
infidels—The Bible teaches us our duty—Reveals to us fu-
turity—The Bible shows the way to be saved.

THE winter of which I am writing was very
severe. On the morning following the conversation just related, the ground was covered with a
deep snow, so that the boys were forced to remain
in the house. This gave their uncle a good opportunity to teach them many useful things. When
they arose from breakfast, he conducted the two
brothers into his study, and said, " Well, my young
friends, you see there is no out-door amusement
for you to-day. You must make yourselves con-
tented with the company of an old man, in the
house. And let me say to you, we ought to be
thankful that we have a roof over our heads.
Many poor creatures, on this cold day, have no
dwelling-place, and scarcely any clothing. The
snow, which keeps us in the house, is useful to the
fields of grain. The farmers tell us, that in winters when no snow falls, the grain is often injured
The snow and the rain are both wisely and merci-
fully sent, in their season, by the Creator."

Ernest. I have heard it said that it never rains in Egypt.

Uncle. That is true, to a great extent. Neither rain nor snow ever falls in that country, unless on some very rare occasion. As to snow, they do not know what it is. The great river Nile, by overflowing its banks, waters the earth, and makes rain unnecessary. Look at the map. This is one of the most wonderful countries in the world. When Greece was a barbarous region, and when there was no such city as Rome, thousands of years before America or even Great Britain was discovered by civilized men, Egypt was a great kingdom. You have heard of the pyramids. No one

knows when they were built, or by whom, or for what purpose.

Ernest. Are there no histories of Egypt?

Uncle. The oldest histories have perished, thou-

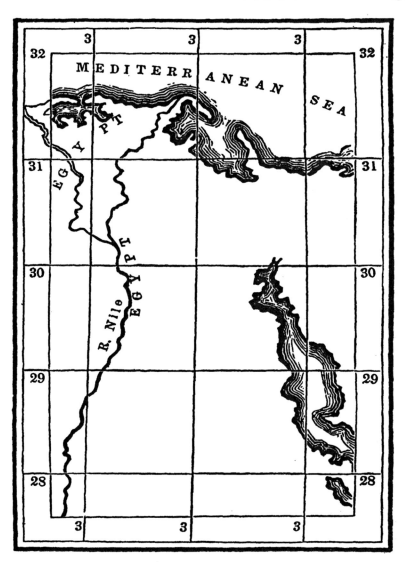

.s ands of years ago.   The first we read about Egypt
is in the Scriptures.

Hilary. Why, is the Bible so old as that?

Uncle. The books of Moses contain the earliest history in the world ; and the Bible is the oldest book in the world. This is one thing which renders it so interesting. No other book can tell us any thing about the creation of the world. But the Bible gives us God's own account of the way in which all things were first made. It tells us how the whole human family descended from one pair. It relates to us the destruction of the world by a flood of water. It informs us how the sons of Noah and their descendants settled the various parts of the earth.

Ernest. I thought some of the Greek and Latin books were very ancient.

Uncle. So they are, but not to be compared to the books of Moses. *Homer* is the oldest Greek poet, but no one pretends that he lived earlier than the year nine hundred and fifty before Christ, and that is only about the time of king Asa. *Herodotus* is the oldest Greek historian, and he lived much later still, about four hundred and fifty years before Christ, that is about the time of Nehemiah.

Hilary. Should we not know any thing about these old times, if we had no Bible ?

Uncle. We should have no certain knowledge. No one could tell the age of the human race, without the Bible. We should have nothing but the ridiculous fables of the heathen, which boys read in Greek and Latin books, and which are too ridiculous to be mentioned. But, my dear boys, this history is but a small part of what this blessed book contains. It is written by the inspiration of the all-wise God. All that is in it is true. But, more than this, all that is in it is *most wise.* It is the book of wisdom. All the wise men on the earth could not produce such a book.

Hilary. Our teacher says that Socrates was a very wise man.

Uncle. He was wise for a heathen; but any Sunday-school child in America, who has been well taught, knows more about God than Socrates did. And the Bible makes the difference. Solomon was a wise king, and he says, " He that walketh with the wise shall be wise." That is, if you want to get wisdom, you must keep company with those who have it. Now if you knew that the very wisest man in the world was going to open a school, would you not like to go to him to be his scholars ?

Ernest. Yes, because I should know that he would never make any mistakes, or teach me any thing wrong.

Hilary. Yes, and if he was so wise, he would teach us the very best things, and would not teach us useless things.

Uncle. Then you ought, for this very reason,

to learn from the Bible. When you read the Bible, you are reading the wisdom of the wisest men. Yes, you are reading the wisdom of the all-wise God. It is just as if you conversed with the wisest of all teachers. This book will never lead you into mistakes; it will never teach you any thing wrong. It will teach you the very best things, in the very best way. It will never teach you any thing trifling, vain, or useless.

Ernest. But is there not a great deal of wisdom in other books ?

Uncle. I do not despise other books. I read many of them, and they help me to understand the Scriptures. But they do not tell me how my soul is to be saved. And besides, all the true knowledge which is in the world about God and about religion, comes from God. It was revealed by him. And if we had no Bible, we should have hardly any of it. Much of the wisdom of the heathens was learned from the Jews, who had the Scriptures.

Ernest. Do you think, if we had no Bible, we should be heathen ?

Uncle. Certainly ; either heathen or infidels. We should be either idolaters or atheists. This is just the fact where the Bible has never been known. The people are " without God." Those fine writers, whose works you read at school, such as Homer and Virgil, were heathen. The

Greeks had thirty thousand gods. The Romans were as bad.

Hilary. That is very strange! Why, had they no more sense than this? Any little child knows better now.

Uncle. Yes, any Christian child. But, Hilary, you yourself would not know any better, if you had not received it from the Scriptures. I have been in countries where the people know nothing about the true God; they worshipped hundreds of horrid images. This was because they had no Bible.

Ernest. But surely, my dear uncle, you think that the Chaldeans, Egyptians, and the Greeks had some wisdom.

Uncle. Yes, my son; you are right. These ancient nations had learned men among them. The Chaldeans used to live in their wide-spread plains, where they could see the heavenly bodies with ease; and so they became astronomers. But take notice, they worshipped these very things. They adored the sun, the moon, and the stars, and denied the one true God. And the Greeks worshipped dead men whom they called heroes, and false gods whom they described as abominably wicked. And the Egyptians worshipped hawks, serpents, cats, crocodiles, monkeys; yes, and even the leeks and onions in their gardens.

Ernest. O, horrible!

Hilary. They were no better than fools.

Uncle. Such fools we should be, if God had not in infinite mercy given us his inspired truth. The wise heathen were fools in these great matters. So the apostle Paul says of them, "Professing themselves to be wise, they became fools, and changed the glory of the incorruptible God into an image made like to corruptible man, and to birds, and four-footed beasts, and creeping things." Rom. i. 22, 23.

Ernest. I heard a Mr. Bald say that nobody needs the Bible now.

Uncle. Why not?

Ernest. He said that there were wise men who could give us as much light as the Bible. He said that he knew people whom he called philosophers, and that they could tell us every thing we need know about our duty, and the way to be happy.

Uncle. This was foolish and wicked talk. If this Mr. Bald had been born in China, he would be a heathen. Why is he not a heathen?

Hilary. Because he lives in a Christian land.

Uncle. What gives more light to this Christian land—more than there is in China?

Hilary. It is the Bible.

Uncle. Then does not Mr. Bald get much of his light and knowledge from the Bible?

Ernest. Yes; for if there had been no Bible, he would have been no better than the Chinese. It is the Bible which makes his philosophers know the little they do know.

Uncle. A man once took a lantern, and put a lamp into it, and lighted it, and set it on a post in the middle of a field. Then he called his wife and children, and said to them, " *What a wonderful light!* Look, you can see all the trees and houses for a mile around!" His wife smiled, and said, " Yes, but the sun is shining with all his glory, for it is noonday."

Ernest. The man was silly.

Uncle. Yes; he was almost an idiot. He thought his lantern made the day. But infidel philosophers, like Mr. Bald, are quite as silly. They make speeches, and write books, and say, " What a wonderful philosophy we have! What a light!" and all the while it is the Bible which makes the light, and gives them the little knowledge they possess.

Ernest. Mr. Bald does not do his duty, even if he does know what it is. For I heard him curse and swear.

Uncle. This is the reason why most infidels hate the Bible; they hate the pure law of God which it contains. They do not wish to do their duty. The Bible tells us what we owe to God

Our *duty* is what God requires of us. It is hard to find this out without revelation.

Ernest. Sometimes I do not know whether what I am doing is right or wrong.

Uncle. If God were to speak in a voice of thunder from heaven, and say, " *This is the way, walk ye in it,*" you would at once know what your duty is. Now God has done as much as this: for in the Scriptures he has given us a rule to direct us how to please him. The Bible tells us plainly what we must do, and what we must not do. This is what no heathen philosopher, and no proud infidel, could tell us.

Ernest. I suppose the heathen did not know what becomes of people when they die.

Uncle. They could only guess. They had a hundred different notions about the world to come. Some thought the soul died with the body. Some thought the soul passed from one body to another, through a great number of animals. Some thought there was a place under the earth where the good were happy, and where the wicked were tormented. Many of them wished for immortality, but could not be sure of it. It is this sacred volume which explains the great secret. You can nowhere else find it explained. Here you learn how to overcome the fear of death. Here you see death conquered. Here you have an account given of heaven and hell, of judgment and eternity. Is not this then the most important book in the world ?

Ernest. Yes, indeed : I see it to be so. And I think there is one thing more you might have said.

Uncle. What is that ?

Ernest. The Scriptures tell us how to get to heaven.

Uncle. You say well. THE WAY TO BE SAVED is the great thing in which every human being is concerned. Here you learn the way. Christ is the way, the truth, and the life. The Holy Scriptures explain to us how Jesus came as a Saviour. Life and immortality are brought to light by the gospel. Only the Scriptures show us how we may find pardon for our sins. This is the glory of the whole book.

Hilary. But does the Old Testament tell about Christ ?

Uncle. Yes, my dear boy. The Old Testament is full of instructions about Christ. These are not so clear as those in the New Testament, but the New Testament shows us the meaning of the Old. All the sacrifices were signs of the sacrifice of Christ. The prophets prophesied of Christ. And " Jesus Christ is the sum and substance of the Scriptures."

After these remarks, uncle Austin arose, and told the boys that he wished to spend an hour or two in reading. He therefore gave them permission to go into the parlour, and amuse themselves with such exercises as they could take within doors.

Ernest and Hilary played until they were fatigued, and then sat down to talk. It was very natural for them to speak of what their uncle had said.

Hilary. I do not wonder that they call him the *Bible man*, for uncle seems to think of nothing else.

Ernest. But this does not keep him from doing a great deal of good. There are many poor families around Oakdale whom he visits every week. When the neighbours are sick, he supplies them with food and medicine.

Hilary. He ought to have been a minister.

Ernest. People can do a great deal of good without being ministers. Some persons would not listen to what uncle Austin says, if they knew him to be a minister. But now, when they know that he is a rich old gentleman, they attend to what he teaches them. He has three Sunday-schools in this neighbourhood.

Hilary. Surely he does not teach them himself!

Ernest. No, not exactly. He set them up, and persuaded some of the pious young people to become teachers. Then he gave them little libraries to begin with, and every Lord's-day he visits some one of them.

Hilary. Now I am sure that the Bible does not make any one dull or cross. Uncle Austin is the very kindest old gentlemen I ever saw. Ernest, I think we must read a little in the Bible every day.

Ernest. Wait a little; if you think so now, you will think so much more after you have been here a few days. But I hear uncle's little bell ringing. John is going to get his horse. We must run and help to get him ready for riding out.

CHAPTER IV.

Divisions of the Bible—Into Testaments—Meaning of the word
Bible—Meaning of the word Testament—Names by which
the Bible is known—Apocrypha—Original languages of Scripture—The Hebrew—The Greek—The Bible written at various times—Made up of many books—Number of these—
Divisions of the Old Testament—Historical, doctrinal, poetical, and prophetical books—Form of ancient books—Hebrew
writing—Service of the synagogues.

ANOTHER day came, and it was a very agreeable
day for the boys, for they had a house full of their
young cousins, who were invited to dine with them.
They enjoyed many sports and many conversations
among themselves, and their uncle came into their
gay circle, now and then, with a smiling countenance, making them useful presents, and giving
them good advice. But though the day was so
pleasant, yet Ernest and Hilary agreed that they
should be glad for the next day to come, that they
might hear something more in the study.

The next morning, as usual, they were called
into the study. A large and beautiful book lay
upon the table in the middle of the room. Uncle
Austin said to them, "Boys, open that book.

Ernest. It is a beautiful Bible ! It is the largest
I ever saw.

Hilary. The print is so large, that one could almost read it across the room.

Uncle. I brought it with me from England. It was printed at Oxford. I find it very pleasant for my old eyes. Now look at it, and tell me into what parts it is divided.

Ernest. O, I know that very well. There are two parts—the *Old Testament* and the *New Testament.*

Uncle. Yes; these are the two great divisions of the Scriptures. Both these together make up the *Bible.*

Hilary. But we speak of the *Bible* and the *Testament.* Is the Testament a part of the Bible?

Uncle. It is a vulgar error. Ignorant people call the *Old Testament* the *Bible;* and they call the *New Testament* the *Testament.*

Ernest. They ought to say the *Bible* for the whole; the *Old Testament* for the first part, and the *New Testament* for the other part. Hereafter I shall try to remember.

Uncle. Take notice, there are two Testaments, and these two Testaments make the Bible. Instead of saying *the Testament*, say *the New Testament.*

Ernest. But what does *Bible* mean?

Uncle. *Bible* is a word derived from the Greek. *Biblia* in Greek means *the Books.* *Biblia* in Latin means the same. These words are in the plural

number. The English word *Bible* means *the
Book*. We call the Scriptures *the Book*, because
they are the best of books.

Ernest. Are there not other names ?

Uncle. Yes ; the Bible is called the *Scriptures*,
or writings : the *Holy Scriptures*, or holy writings,
because it was written by inspiration of God's Holy
Spirit. In the Scriptures themselves, we do not
find the name *Bible*. But the common names there
given are *the Scriptures*, the *Law*, (the *Word of
God*.) Turn to Psalm cxix.

Ernest. Here it is ; it has a hundred and seventy-
six verses !

Uncle. Yes ; and every verse has something in
honour of the Scriptures. The psalmist had not
half so much of the Bible as we have, but he loved
what he had. Just see how many names he gives
the law of God in this one psalm. I will read
them. The Law of the Lord—God's Testimo-
nies—Precepts—Statutes—Commandments—Judg-
ments—God's Word, (ver. 9. 11. 16. 25. 41—43.
58. 65. 101. 114. 133. 140. 158. 160, 161. 170 ;)
God's Words—the Law of God's mouth.

Ernest. But some Bibles have another part between the Old and the New Testaments.

Uncle. That is what is called the *Apocrypha.*
It is not inspired. It is no part of God's revelation.
Some of it is good, and some of it is bad ; but it is

not Scripture. Let me ask you a question: Is this the language in which the Bible was written at first?

Ernest. No, sir, I suppose not.

Uncle. Ernest, you surely know in what language the New Testament was written.

Ernest. Yes, sir, in the *Greek* language ; for I have to read the Greek Testament with my teacher.

Uncle. Very well. Then you have only to learn that the rest of the Bible was written in *Hebrew.* These two languages, *Hebrew* and *Greek,* are the two which God chose to give us his revelation in.

Hilary. Why did God select these languages ?

Uncle. *Hebrew* was the language of the patriarchs, and of the Israelites, who were the people of God, and the only people on earth who had a revelation. *Greek* was the language most extensively used in the world at the time of our Saviour. But I shall say more of these things at another time.

Hilary. Was the Old Testament all written by the same person ?

Uncle. O, no; by no means : by more than *twenty* different inspired men. People are apt to fall into a great mistake about this. When they see all in one volume, they think it is all one composition. But the truth is, the Bible is made up of a large number of separate books.

Hilary. Then I suppose they were not written all at once?

Uncle. Not at all. They were written at different times. From the time at which the first book of the Old Testament was written till the time the last book was written, is more than a *thousand* years; and from the first book in the Bible till the last, there is more than *nineteen hundred* years.

Hilary. Is it possible! Then the book of Genesis is almost two thousand years older than the book of Revelation!

Uncle. Exactly so. You see that you might take out each of these separate parts, and make a little volume of it by itself. It would be a little library of itself. There you would have some books by Moses, some by Solomon, some by Ezra, and so on. Now look at this Bible, and tell me how many books it contains.

Hilary. I will count them. There are just sixty-six, beginning with Genesis and ending with Revelation.

Ernest. Yes; there are *thirty-nine* in the Old Testament, and *twenty-seven* in the New Testament.

Uncle. Now remember what you learned just now. The first division we make is into the two Testaments. This is very simple; you cannot forget it. But let us take the *Old Testament*, and see if we cannot make some convenient division of it.

Ernest. Yes, into thirty-nine separate books.

Uncle. Very true ; but we can make a division more easy to be remembered. Some of these thirty-nine books relate histories : let us call these *historical.* Some of them are poems, like the Psalms, or books of instruction, like Ecclesiastes : let us call these *doctrinal or poetical.* The remainder are predictions of things to come : let us call these *prophetical.*

Ernest. See if I understand you. The Old Testament is divided into three parts :

I. *The Historical Books.*

II. *The Doctrinal or Poetical Books.*

III. *The Prophetical Books.*

Hilary. Will you inform me which are in each of these divisions ?

Uncle. The *historical books* are seventeen. namely, 1. Genesis. 2. Exodus. 3. Leviticus. 4. Numbers. 5. Deuteronomy. 6. Joshua. 7. Judges. 8. Ruth. 9. The first book of Samuel. 10. The second book of Samuel. 11. The first book of Kings. 12. The second book of Kings. 13. The first book of Chronicles. 14. The second book of Chronicles. 15. Ezra. 16. Nehemiah. 17. Esther.

The *doctrinal or poetical books* are five:
namely, 1. Job. 2. Psalms. 3. Proverbs. 4. Ecclesiastes. 5. The Song of Solomon.

The *prophetical books* are equal in number to
the historical, seventeen: namely, 1. Isaiah. 2. Jeremiah. 3. Lamentations. 4. Ezekiel. 5. Daniel.
6. Hosea. 7. Joel. 8. Amos. 9. Obadiah. 10. Jonah. 11. Micah. 12. Nahum. 13. Habakkuk.
14. Zephaniah. 15. Haggai. 16. Zechariah.
17. Malachi.

Ernest. Can we divide them any further?

Uncle. It is not very necessary. But you may
as well learn now, as at any other time, that the
first five historical books were written by Moses.
They are sometimes called *the books of Moses.*
The Jews called them the *Law.* They are also
called *the Pentateuch*, a Greek word, meaning
" five books," or " five volumes."

The *prophetical* books are also divided into the
greater and the *lesser.* The *greater prophets* are
the first four, — Isaiah, Jeremiah, Ezekiel, and
Daniel. The *lesser* or *minor* prophets are all the
rest.

Ernest. Were these books in separate volumes?

Uncle. The Jews always had the Pentateuch in
one book, which they called the Book of the Law.
But I shall show you that the ancient books were
not like our's. They were *rolls of skin*, and looked

more like a map upon rollers, than any thing else.

Hilary. Did you not say that all the Old Testament was written in Hebrew?

Uncle. I did. But there is a little exception to be made. There is a language called *Chaldee,* which was spoken in Chaldea, where the Israelites were carried away captive. A very small part of the Bible is in this language. But the Chaldee parts are only a few pages in all.*

Hilary. I wish to see what the Hebrew looks like.

---

* The following parts are in Chaldee:—Daniel ii. 4 vii. Ezra iv. 8—vi. 18; vii. 12—26. Jer. x. 11.

Uncle. Very well ; let me write down the first verse in the Bible in Hebrew for you.

בראשית ברא אלהים את השמים ואת הארץ׃

There you have it. But you can see it better in a Hebrew Bible. Take this Hebrew Bible, and examine it, with the points.

Hilary. Uncle, the title-page seems to be at the end.

Uncle. What you call the end is the beginning. The Hebrews always began at the *right hand* of the page when they wrote, and not, as we do, at the *left hand.* So that the first page is where the last would be in an English book.

Ernest. Whereabouts is the Hebrew language spoken ?

Uncle. Pure Hebrew is not spoken anywhere on earth at this time. It is read by the Jews, and by many learned Christians.

Ernest. But it was spoken in old times ?

Uncle. Yes ; it was spoken by the Hebrews, and especially by the Israelites. Many good men believe that Adam and Eve spake Hebrew, and that it was Hebrew which God taught them.

Ernest. Then it is the oldest of all languages.

Uncle. It is. We do not know of any older language. Many languages are derived from it. It was spoken by all the people of Palestine ; by

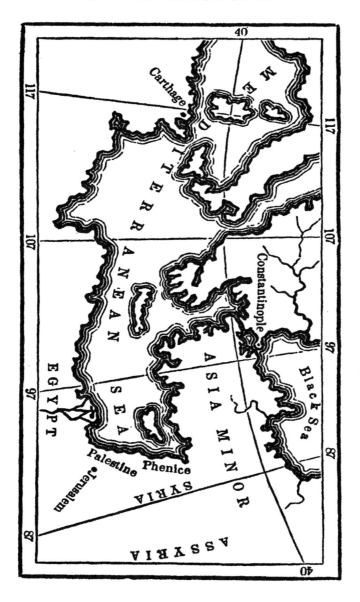

the Phenicians, north of Palestine; by the Canaan-
ites; and, it is said, by the Carthaginians, who
were originally Phenicians. But, besides this, I
have no doubt it was once the language of the great
nations all around Palestine. During the seventy
years of captivity, the Hebrews lost much of their
own language, and borrowed much from the Chaldee, which was very nearly like Hebrew. But
the difference was such, that the Bible was explained in Chaldee for the use of the Jews.

Hilary. Do the Jews understand Hebrew?

Uncle. At the present day, only a part of the
Jews understand Hebrew perfectly. There are
learned men among them who are great Hebrew
scholars; but many of them read the words without knowing very well what they mean. Have
you ever been at the Jewish synágogue?

Hilary. Yes, sir, we have both been to the
synagogue in New York. We heard them read
and sing, for several hours, in a very strange language.

Uncle. That was Hebrew. Every Jew is taught
in his childhood to pronounce the language. They
honour the Old Testament, and read some part of
it in the synagogues every Sabbath. They have
done this for two thousand years. They have the
Pentateuch divided into fifty-four sections, and they
read one of these every Saturday.

Ernest. Do they read nothing but the *Law?*

Uncle. Yes; they read in the prophets, also. About a hundred and sixty years before Christ, Antiochus forbade them to read the law. They therefore took fifty-four sections of the prophets, and read them. When they were again allowed to read the law, they continued to read the prophets also.

Hilary. When I go again to the synagogue, I will pay more attention to what they do.

Uncle. That will be right. But now we must think of some other business for the morning. I am afraid you think all this very dry. But you should remember that it is very useful. And after a few more conversations, I shall have something much more entertaining to teach you.

The boys thanked their good uncle, and left his study, to go and prepare for a visit they were about to make to the neighbouring village.

CHAPTER V.

The New Testament—Why written in Greek—Period between the two Testaments—Divisions of the New Testament—Historical, doctrinal, and prophetical books—Writers of the different books—Table of the writers and dates—Advantage of reading the Bible in the original—How the Moslems read the Koran—The word Gospel—The catholic epistles.

THE next conversation was about the second great division of the Bible, or, the *New Testament.* The boys were seated in the study before a good fire, when their uncle began thus:

Uncle. Yesterday I explained to you several things about the Old Testament. To-day I mean to talk about the New Testament.

Ernest. What is the meaning of *Testament?*

Uncle. It means *covenant.* This second part of the Bible is called the *New Covenant* by the early Christian writers, just as the former part was called the Old Covenant. You will find the words used by Paul, in 2 Cor. iii. 6—18. Whether in this place the apostle means the *books,* or only the precepts and truths of the books, is not agreed.

Ernest. Why were the Scriptures called *Covenants,* or *Testaments?*

Uncle. Because they contain the revelation of God's dealings with mankind, which are often called covenants. Especially the New Testament contains the covenant of our salvation. The word *testament* often means a *last will*, or the writing by which a man leaves any thing to his heirs. This book contains an account of the Christian inheritance. The New Testament was written in the Greek language.

Hilary. Why was it not written in Hebrew?

Uncle. For two reasons. First, because at the time of our Saviour the Hebrew language was very little spoken. Secondly, because the revelation of God was now to be given, not to the Hebrews alone, but to all nations.

Hilary. Did not Christ and the apostles speak Hebrew?

Uncle. They no doubt knew the Hebrew; but the common language of Palestine, at that time, was a dialect of Hebrew; that is a sort of Hebrew much altered. It has sometimes been called *Syro-Chaldaic*, because it was between Syriac and Chaldee. But the New Testament was not written in this dialect, because it was understood in only a small part of the earth.

Hilary. But why was the Greek language chosen?

Uncle. Because it was read and spoken all over the Roman empire. You must know that at that time the Romans were the masters of all the civil-

ized world.   They had conquered a large part of
Europe, Asia, and Africa.   Palestine was under
their power.

Ernest.   But was not *Latin* the language of the
Romans ?   Why was not the New Testament written in *Latin ?*

Uncle.   Latin was the Roman language, and it
was spoken in Italy ; but Greek was more commonly used in all other parts of the Roman empire.
Every educated person learned Greek, even at
Rome.   Juvenal tells us that ladies spoke Greek.
Cicero says the Greek was read in almost all nations.   If any other language had been used, these
writings could not have been understood except in
one narrow region.

Ernest.   Does the New Testament begin just at
the time that the Old Testament ends ?

Uncle.   No ; there is a period between the two
of more than four hundred years.   Some very important events happened during this period.   You
must know something of this in order to understand the Scriptures.   It was during this period
that Asia was invaded by Alexander the Great ;
that Judea was invaded by Antiochus, and that
Palestine was subdued by the Romans.

Ernest.   There are *twenty-seven* books in the
New Testament.   Now can we divide these, as
we did those of the Old ?

Uncle. Yes ; and we may use the very same division. Some of these books relate the history of Christ and his apostles : let us call these *historical.* Some of them are letters containing Christian doctrine : let us call these *doctrinal.* The only book left is the last in the Bible, which is a book of predictions : let us call this *prophetical.*

Hilary. I will repeat. The New Testament is divided into three parts :

I. *The Historical Books.*

II. *The Doctrinal Books.*

III. *The Prophetical Book.*

Uncle. Now open your Bible. The *historical* books are five ; namely, the Gospels, and the Acts of the Apostles.

The *doctrinal* books are twenty-one ; namely, 1. The Epistle to the Romans. 2. The first Epistle to the Corinthians. 3. The second Epistle to the Corinthians. 4. The Epistle to the Galatians. 5. The Epistle to the Ephesians. 6. The Epistle to the Philippians. 7. The Epistle to the Colossians. 8. The first Epistle to the Thessalonians. 9. The second Epistle to the Thessalonians. 10. The first Epistle to Timothy. 11. The second Epistle to Timothy. 12. The Epistle to Titus. 13. The Epistle to Philemon. 14. The Epistle to the Hebrews. 15. The Epistle of James. 16. The first Epistle of Peter. 17. The second Epistle of Peter.

18. The first Epistle of John. 19. The second Epistle of John. 20. The third Epistle of John. 21. The Epistle of Jude.

The *prophetical* book is the Revelation of John.

Ernest. How many different persons were employed in writing these twenty-seven books?

Uncle. Eight persons.

Hilary. Were they all apostles?

Uncle. All except *Mark* and *Luke*, and these were constant companions of the apostles. Mark attended on Peter, and Luke on Paul.

Hilary. Who wrote the most?

Uncle. The apostle Paul wrote more than any. Next to him, the apostle John. Next, Luke. Then Matthew, Mark, Peter, James, and Jude.

Ernest. Are the books placed in our Bibles in the order in which they were written?

Uncle. No; you would greatly mistake if you took up this notion. It is a common error. The epistles are arranged after the histories. But some of the epistles were written first. First come the epistles of Paul, and then those of the other apostles. And the epistles of Paul are arranged according to their length; first that to the Romans, which is his longest; and last, that to Philemon, which is his shortest. The Epistle to the Hebrews is not, indeed, taken into this arrangement, because it has not the apostle Paul's name.

Ernest. This is new to me. Are the other epistles arranged in the same way?

Uncle. Very much in the same way; for James is rather longer than the First of Peter; and the epistles of John are arranged agreeably to their length.

Hilary. Did our Saviour write any thing himself?

Uncle. We have no knowledge of his having written any thing.

Hilary. I suppose that the epistles were written at different times.

Uncle. Yes; and at different places. Learned men differ as to the exact time when each book was written, and we cannot be certain. I will show you a list drawn up according to Dr. Lardner. You will find another calculation in the Union Bible Dictionary, under the word Epistles.

Ernest. Then there are forty-four years between the first and the last book of the New Testament.

Uncle. Yes; if Dr. Lardner is right in his calculation. And you see that it was some time after our Saviour's ascension into heaven that the first of these books was written. Our Saviour ascended in the year 33, and the Epistle to the Thessalonians was written in the year 52.

Hilary. I wish to learn Greek much more than I ever did before.

Books.	Places where written.	Time when written.	Books.	Chaps.	Verses.
Historical Books.					
Matthew	Judea	A.D. 64	1	28	1071
Mark	Rome	64	1	16	678
Luke	Greece	63 or 64	1	24	1151
John	Ephesus	68	1	21	880
Acts	Greece	63 or 64	1	28	1006
Epistles of Paul.					
1 Thessalonians	Corinth	52	1	5	89
2 Thessalonians	Corinth	52	1	3	47
Galatians	Corinth or Ephesus	52 or 53	1	6	149
1 Corinthians	Ephesus	Beginning of 56	1	16	437
1 Timothy	Macedonia	56	1	6	113
Titus	Macedonia, or near it	Before the end of 56	1	3	46
2 Corinthians	Macedonia	October, 57	1	13	256
Romans	Corinth	February, 58	1	16	434
Ephesians	Rome	April, 61	1	6	155
2 Timothy	Rome	May, 61	1	4	83
Philippians	Rome	End of 62	1	4	104
Colossians	Rome	End of 62	1	4	95
Philemon	Rome	End of 62	1	1	25
Hebrews	Rome, or Italy	Spring of 63	1	13	303
The Catholic Epistles.					
James	Judea	61 or 62	1	5	108
1 Peter	Rome	64	1	5	105
2 Peter	Rome	64	1	3	61
1 John	Ephesus	80	1	5	105
2 John	Ephesus	Between 80—90	1	1	13
3 John	Ephesus	Between 80—96	1	1	15
Jude	Unknown	64 or 65	1	1	25
Apocalypse	Patmos, or Ephesus	95 or 96	1	22	405
Total			27	260	7959

Uncle. It is a fine language, and it is particularly useful, because the New Testament is written in it. We call the Hebrew and the Greek the *original languages* of Scripture, because the Bible was originally written in them.

Ernest. Is not a translation into English just as good as the Greek?

Uncle. We ought to be very thankful to God that we have so good a translation; yet no translation can be quite equal to the original. There is always something in the translation which is not in the original; and there is always something in the original which is not in the translation. And therefore it is a good thing to know the original languages.

Hilary. Did you not say that all the Jewish children are taught to read in the Hebrew Bible?

Uncle. Yes; all learn to read the words, and, in some countries, all learn to understand what they read. A Jew would be ashamed not to know the Hebrew letters. And among the Mohammedans, every boy is taught to read the Koran. The *Koran* is the sacred book of all who follow Mohammed. It was written by him in the Arabic language. And though many of the Mohammedans live in countries where the Arabic language is not spoken, yet they all learn to read the Koran in the original.

Ernest. Why might we not learn to read Greek in the same manner?

Uncle. It is not likely that everybody can be persuaded to learn it; nor is it the duty of every one. But many thousands might do so, who now neglect it. People can learn French and Italian, and so they might learn Greek enough to understand the New Testament.

Ernest. I think it must be very delightful to know that you are reading the very words which the inspired men wrote.

Uncle. Yes; it is so, indeed. And I hope you will both be diligent in learning to do so. Then I hope you will begin the Hebrew also. For there is nothing which you ever learn at school half as important as the Holy Scriptures.

Hilary. But before we know Hebrew and Greek, what must we do?

Uncle. You will find enough to do, and that which is very profitable and delightful. You have this blessed English Bible, the very best translation which was ever made, which has, with God's blessing, made so many thousands wise unto salvation. Study this. Learn all about it. Read it every day. Commit portions of it to memory. Believe it. Pray over it. Practise it. And you will then say, as the psalmist said, *O how I love thy law!* it is my meditation all the day. I love thy commandments above gold, yea, above fine gold. The law of thy mouth is better unto me than thousands of gold and silver.

Ernest. There is a question I should like to ask about the names of some of the books. Why are four of the historical books called *Gospels?*

Uncle. The word *gospel* is derived from two Saxon words, *god*—good, and *spel*—word or news; it therefore means *good news.* The Greek word (Euaggelion) which means *good news,* is used to express the glad tidings of Messiah's coming. Matt. xi. 5. Rom. i. 1, 2. The early Christians gave this same name to the small books which contained the history of Christ. These books are those of Matthew, Mark, Luke, and John, which are called the gospels according to these writers; that is, the history of Christ's blessed coming, as recorded by these writers. From the same Greek word is derived the Latin for gospel, *Evangelium;* and from this these writers are called the *Evangelists.*

Ernest. In the table which you showed us, (see page 64,) all the epistles, except those of Paul, are called *catholic* epistles. I do not know what this means.

Uncle. It is a very ancient name, and I am not sure that we know why it was first given. *Catholic* means *universal;* thus the *catholic church* means the *universal church of Christ,* and not the church of Rome. Some think these letters are so called because they were not for *individuals*, but for the universal body of believers. Others think they were so called, from their being *universally received* as Scripture.

Hilary. What is the meaning of *Apocalypse?*

Uncle. It is only the Greek for *Revelation.* And take care not to call this last book *Revelations*, as ignorant people do, but *Revelation;* for it is in the singular number. And now I am sure I have wearied you; so you may make your escape.

CHAPTER VI.

Ancient writing and books—Meaning of the word Volume—Invention of writing—Scrolls—Materials on which books were written. I. Vegetable substances—Leaves of trees—Bark—Wood—Roman tablets—Egyptian papyrus. II. Animal substances—Skins—Parchment—Vellum—Bones—Shells. III. Mineral substances—Lead—Copper—Brass—Silver—Gold—Stone—Bricks.

ON the next day, when Ernest and Hilary went into their uncle's study, they were surprised to see him unrolling a great skin, which looked like a long narrow map.

Uncle. This is not a map, as you might be ready to suppose, but a *book.*

Hilary. A book! Is it possible? Why it has no leaves and no cover. It looks more like a large roll of sheepskin.

Uncle. So it is; nothing more nor less than a large roll of sheepskin; but still it is a book. Have you never heard a book called a *volume?*

Hilary. O, yes; often.

Uncle. Volume means something *rolled up.* In old times books were rolled in this way, and were called *volumes* or *rolls:* but I am going to tell you a great deal more about this. And if you will only be attentive, I think you will be entertained.

Ernest. We will try to be attentive. But before you go on any further, I should like you to tell me who invented books and writing. Do you think Adam could write?

Uncle. That is not revealed to us. Some persons think that Moses was the inventor of writing; this is the common opinion. But I have always thought it much more likely that the art of writing was known long before Moses. I have already told you, however, that the Pentateuch, as Moses' works are called, is the oldest book in existence.

Hilary. Were all the ancient books written on skins like this?

Uncle. Many of them were, but a great variety of articles have been used to write upon; and I am about to give you an account of these. It will help you to understand many parts of the Bible. These articles were of three sorts: 1. *Vegetable* substances; 2. *Animal* substances; 3. *Mineral* substances. I am unable, indeed, to inform you which was the very earliest writing material, but I can tell you of several which were certainly used by the ancients.

FIRST. *The leaves of trees.* In the East Indies the natives at this day write on leaves. In Tanjore and other countries, the *palmyra leaf* is used; and they make the letters with a sharp piece of metal like a bodkin. The people of Ceylon use

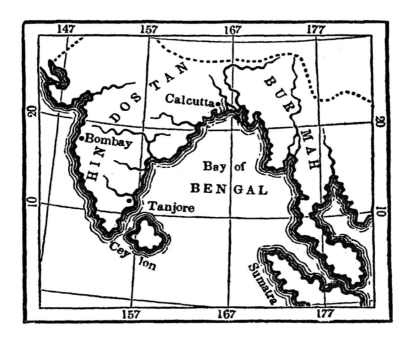

the *palm leaf*, which is of immense size. They cut out slips between one and two feet in length, and when they have smoothed them, they write on them with a steel pencil. They make holes in these, and string them together; and thus they have books. Pliny tells us that this was one of the most ancient ways of writing.

SECONDLY. *The bark of trees and plants.* The Greeks called this BIBLOS, whence the word BIBLIA, whence our word BIBLE. Sometimes they did nothing to the bark but make it smooth. The *phi-lyra*, a sort of linden tree, was much used for this purpose, and even the bark of some oaks. The

Latin word *Liber* means the inner bark of a tree, and also a book. But the ancients learned to prepare this into a sort of paper; by separating the thin layers of bark, laying one on another with some gum or paste, and then pressing them close. This sort of paper was used in France, seven hundred years ago. The great fault of it was that it blotted. The sacred books of the Burmans are sometimes made of thin strips or slices of bamboo, plaited together nicely, so as to make a smooth leaf of the required size. In the island of Suma-

tra, south of Burmah, under the equator, the natives use the bark of trees for writing.

THIRDLY. *Wood itself* has been employed for books. Pliny tells us that table-books of wood were in use before the days of Homer. Before the Chinese had invented their fine paper, they used thin pieces of wood or bamboo, on which they marked with an iron tool. And there are at Oxford some specimens of ancient Arabic writing on boards about two feet long and six inches wide. In Ezekiel xxxvii. 15, the Lord directs the prophet to write on two *sticks*. These were no doubt such tablets of wood. And the writing-table on which Zechariah wrote the name of John the Baptist, was a tablet of wood. Luke i. 63. The ancient people of Britain used to cut the letters on sticks having three or four sides, and these sticks were fixed in a frame. The Danes did the same, and the word Book is derived from the old northern word *Boc*, " beech," because they used beechen boards to write on. In the Apocrypha there is a remarkable proof of the same thing. In second Esdras, chapter fourteenth, verse 24, we read of five men being " ready to write swiftly" on " many *box-trees*," or box-tables. And in verse 44, it is said, " In forty days, they wrote two hundred and four books." The Romans had books of this sort, made of very thin slips of board. And Dr. Shaw tells us, that in Barbary, at the north of Africa, the children at school learn to write on a smooth thin board, daubed over with whiting, which may be easily rubbed off. Thus they learn to read and write at the same time.

Ernest. That is like what I have seen in a Lancasterian school. The little boys had shallow boxes or trays with sand in them, and they made the letters in the sand with a stick, and then rubbed them out again.

Uncle. These wooden tablets were sometimes

covered with a coat of *wax*, and as many as five
or six were occasionally joined together like a
book.   These were very useful when they did not
wish to preserve their writing.

Hilary. Then they answered the same purpose
as our slates.

Uncle. Exactly.   But they likewise wrote long
works on them.   One of Plato's celebrated books,
called the *Republic*, was so written.   They could
write very rapidly on these *waxen tablets*.   Instead
of wood, they sometimes used ivory.   The Romans
constantly carried such tablets with them, or very
rich men were followed by a slave called Tabellarius, who carried the writing materials.   The
Tabellarius often carried letters written on these
waxed boards.   I have seen a French song, written more than four hundred years ago, about **1376**,
which runs thus :

> Some with the antiquated style
> On *waxen tablets* promptly write,
> Others with finer pen the while,
> Form letters lovelier to the sight.

Some French records of that age are still preserved on such tables.   I will explain presently
how they marked on them.

Ernest. But had these ancient people no such
thing as paper ?

Uncle. They had. Let me therefore say,

FOURTHLY, Paper was used for writing. The Egyptians were the first to use paper.* It was made of the celebrated papyrus, or a sort of flag or bulrush which used to grow along the Nile, though at present it is found chiefly in Syria, on the Euphrates, and in India.† The stem of the papyrus is composed of long fibres or strings. It is naked and slender, except at the top, where there is a bunch or plume of leaves, not unlike hairs. It rises sometimes to the height of twenty feet. Pliny gives us a very particular account of the manner in which the ancients made paper from this reed; and Bruce, a modern traveller, has explained many points concerning which we were before ignorant.

Ernest. Is our word *paper* from this name *papyrus* ?

Uncle. It is. This is the first manufactured paper of which we have any account. It was made from the inner bark of the stem, by dividing it into thin slices or skins, as large as possible. The middle skins or films were the most valuable. They laid these slender slips or slices flat on a

---

* See cut on page 35.

† See the beautiful engraving under article *Bulrush,* in BIBLE NATURAL HISTORY, by American Sunday-school Union.

table, edge to edge; over these they laid a layer crossing the former layer at right angles. They put as many layers as they thought needful, and moistened the whole with water. Then they pressed it with great weights. The gummy juice of the papyrus caused the slips to stick together into a firm sheet. When the juice was not sufficiently adhesive, they used wheaten paste. After the sheets had been under press, they beat it with mallets, which smoothed and flattened it. This was the famous *Egyptian* paper.

Hilary. Was it used anywhere but in Egypt?

Uncle. Yes; it was exported into various countries, especially into Italy. About the time of our Saviour's birth, it was one of the chief articles of Egyptian and Roman commerce.

Ernest. How long ago did it go out of use?

Uncle. I cannot inform you with certainty. I think we may say about the middle of the seventh century, when the Saracens subdued Egypt, and thus broke up the paper trade.

Ernest. Are any books of this sort left?

Uncle. Nearly eighteen hundred writings on papyrus have been found in the ruins of Herculaneum. And Bruce, the great traveller, brought from Thebes, in Egypt, a fine specimen. I will read to you what he says: " The boards," or covers, " are of papyrus root, covered first with the coarse pieces of the paper, and then with leather, in the same manner as it would be done now. It is a book one would call a small folio, rather than by any other name. The letters are strong, deep, black, and apparently written with a reed, as is practised by the Egyptians and Abyssinians still. It is written on both sides."

Hilary. Then the papyrus books were not rolls ?

Uncle. This book of Bruce's was not. But more commonly they were rolled. I have myself examined a roll, taken out of the case of a mummy, several thousand years old. It was exhibited in Philadelphia in 1833. Most of the mummies have such rolls.

Ernest. But are you not to tell us something about writing on skins ?

Uncle. I will do so. FIFTHLY. *The skins of animals* were used for writing materials. *Herodotus,* the earliest Greek historian, who lived about four hundred and fifty years before Christ, tells us that the Phenicians wrote on sheep-skins. This was one of the earliest inventions in the way of writing. Skins are strong and lasting. In the Pentateuch we find it said of a certain trial : " And the priest shall write these curses *in a book,* and he shall *blot them out* with water." Num. v. 23 Now this writing must have been on something stronger than paper, which would go to pieces if dipped in water. I think it must have been some sort of skin or leather. We know that the Hebrews were able to dress skins in some ways, because they were much used in the tabernacle; and they could probably dress them so as to take ink or paint.

Ernest. Is not *parchment* made of skins?

Uncle. It is. But in very ancient times this beautiful article was unknown. The skins which they used were rougher and coarser, like the roll which lies on the table.

Hilary. What is *parchment?*

Uncle. *Parchment* is commonly made of the skins of sheep or goats. The sort which is called *vellum* is very fine and delicate, and is made of the skins of the very youngest calves.

Hilary. When was parchment invented?

Uncle. The common opinion is, that it was invented by *Eumenes*, king of Pergamus, about two hundred years before Christ. Pergamus was a great city of Asia Minor, now called Bergamo. It was famous for a library of 200,000 volumes. Ptolemy, king of Egypt, prevented this king from having any *papyrus*, and he therefore adopted this sort of skin. It was called *pergamena* because it was made at *Pergamus*; and *parchment* is derived from *pergamena*. Asses' skin was also used, likewise ivory, and even fish skins. And perhaps you will be amused to hear that old Cleanthes, a Greek philosopher, who was too poor to buy paper, used to write his master Zeno's lectures on *shells* and *beef bones.* Gibbon says that the Koran of Mohammed was taken down by his disciples not only on palm leaves, but the *shoulder bones of mutton.* But you need not reckon the shells or the bones.

Ernest. Did not the ancients sometimes engrave letters on plates of metal?

Uncle. They did. The SIXTH material I shall mention is *lead.* Read Job xix. 24. Montfaucon, a very learned man, bought at Rome, in 1669, a book with leaden leaves. In Greek and Latin writers you will often find, that poems and even laws were engraven on very thin pieces of lead.

SEVENTH. Brass or copper was also used. Dr. Buchanan found among the Jews of India several tables of brass, containing deeds for the land which they owned. The old Roman laws were sometimes thus written. In 1444, seven or eight brass tablets with old Italian writings were dug up in Italy.

EIGHTH. *More precious metals.* I have read that the ancient records of France were on *silver* tablets. In 1636, the Dutch received a letter in Arabic, from an East Indian prince, on tablets of *gold.*

Ernest. But I should think that *stone* would have been used much earlier. The law of God was on tables of stone.

Uncle. Yes, you are right.   In all ancient countries we find monuments of stone, with writings upon them.   Sometimes they cut the letters very deep, and filled them up with lime or cement.   At Rome there is a book with the leaves of thin *marble.*   Job says, "O that my words were now written!   O that they were printed (or graven) in a book!   That they were graven with an iron pen, and lead, in the *rock* forever!"   Job xix. 24. When God called Moses up into Sinai, he said, "I will give thee *tables of stone,* and a law, and commandments which I have written."   Ex. xxiv. 12.   These were "written with the finger of God," (Ex. xxxi. 18,) and are the same which Moses cast out of his hands and broke. Ex. xxxii. 19. The Lord afterwards said to him "Hew thee two *tables of stone* like unto the first." Ex. xxxiv. 1. On these he again inscribed the law.   The people also received a command : "It shall be on the day when ye shall pass over Jordan unto the land which the Lord thy God giveth thee, that thou shalt set thee up *great stones,* and plaster them with plaster : and thou shalt write upon them all the words of this law." Deut. xxvii. 1—8.

NINTH. *Bricks.* These are found among the ruins of Babylon.

TENTH. *Linen, cotton,* and *silk.* Linen books have been found in the caves of Egypt. Livy mentions the like. There is a silk book preserved in the Harleian library in England. And in Rome there is a manuscript of the prophets on silk.

Ernest. Let me see if I can repeat the different things you have mentioned.

Uncle. Begin with those made of *trees* or *plants.*

Ernest. Writing materials made of trees or plants were five : (1.) *Leaves ;* (2.) *Bark ;* (3.) *Wood ;* (4.) *Linen* or *cotton ;* (5.) *Papyrus.*

Uncle. Let Hilary mention those procured from *animals.*

Hilary. Writing materials procured from animals were two : (1.) *Skins,* or *parchment,* or *vellum ;* (2.) *Silk.*

Uncle. And then those which are from the *mineral world* are : (1.) *Metallic plates,* of gold, silver, brass, copper, or lead ; and, (2.) Stone. And now we may stop, as we have discovered something about the articles *on which* the ancients wrote. Next we shall try to find out something about their *pens,* their *ink,* and the fashion of their *books.*

CHAPTER VII.

Ancient writing and books, continued—Ancient pens—Reeds
Introduction of quill-pens—Roman inkstands—Ancient ink—
Hair pencils—Iron pens—The stylus—Waxen tablets—Man-
ner of binding ancient books—Synagogue rolls—Rollers—
Sealed books—Cases for books—Scribes or amanuenses.

IF the reader is not weary of this subject, he may
find in this chapter an account of the conversation
which uncle Austin had with his nephews, about
the sorts of books which were used in old times.
And this is by no means a useless kind of knowledge, because it throws light on many parts of the
Holy Scriptures.

When the boys went, as usual, into the study,
they found that their good uncle was ready for
them. He was sitting near a small table, on which
he had spread a number of drawings, and several
curiosities which he had picked up in his travels.

Uncle. Which of you can tell what this is, which
I hold in my hand ?

Hilary. It looks something like the reeds which
I have seen in tobacco-pipes.

Uncle. It is something of that sort, indeed. It
is a reed for writing. The Arabs and Turks constantly write with a reed of this sort. The an-

cients used a reed when they wrote upon skins, cotton, linen, or paper.

Ernest. Had they no quills to make pens of?

Uncle. Quills have long been used in Europe, but when they were first introduced I cannot tell. Those of geese, swans, peacocks, crows, and pelicans have been employed. The first mention I can find of a pen, is about A. D. 636. They were not known, however, in very ancient times, nor by any of the scriptural writers. Where you find the word *pen* in the English Bible, it means either a rod of some kind, or a sharp instrument of metal. Even after pens were introduced, reeds were used for writing very large or ornamental letters. Here is a Persian manuscript, see how broad and free the long flourished letters are.

Hilary. Can it be possible that this was written! It is as regular as printing.

Uncle. No printing (except lithography) can at all imitate the elegance of oriental manuscripts. And some of the Jews' rolls in their synagogues are still more regular and beautiful. Here is a little drawing I made from a picture which was found in Herculaneum. These pictures are at least seventeen hundred years old.

Ernest. Then they will show us exactly the sort of articles which were common among the old Romans.

Uncle. Exactly so. This is an *inkstand,* with a *reed* lying on it, ready for use.

Hilary. The picture is precisely like the reed yon have in your hand.

Uncle. The *ink* which was used with these reeds was very different from ours. Pliny describes various sorts. The most common was made of lampblack, soot, or charcoal, with water and sometimes a little gum ; so that it was much more like shoe-blacking than ink. Printing ink gives you some idea of it. They frequently used a *hair pencil* to make the letters with, as the Chinese do now. The liquor of the *sepia* or black fish was used by the later Romans. The Hebrews, like other eastern nations, used many colours besides black for their writing. But the Greek word for ink in the New Testament signifies black, and so does the Hebrew word in Jer. xxxvi. 18. By referring to the UNION BIBLE DICTIONARY, art. *Book,* you will find another picture from Herculaneum. It represents an *inkhorn* or standish, in which there are two partitions.

Ernest. And you will see also the reed, already cut and sharpened.

Uncle. When they made inscriptions on stone or metal, it was done with a chisel or graver, called in the Bible *a pen of iron.* Sometimes these were sharpened with a diamond at the end, like the instrument which glaziers employ to cut glass. Job xix. 24. Jeremiah says : " The sin of Judah is written with a *pen of iron,* and with the *point of a diamond :* it is graven upon the table of their heart." Jer. xvii. 1. Pliny mentions these diamond points as having been long in use.

Hilary. How did they write on the waxed tablets ?

Uncle. With a hard instrument called a *stylus* or *style.* This was broad at the top and pointed at the bottom. When they wished to rub out, they just turned the other end and made the wax smooth again.

Hilary. Of what were the styles made ?

Uncle. Sometimes of iron or steel; sometimes of wood, brass, ivory, silver, or even gold. They were used as daggers. *Cesar* drew his style and wounded Cassius. The emperor *Claudius* was so much in dread of being assassinated, that he would not let the scribes or public writers bring their styles into his presence. *Cassianus,* a Christian schoolmaster, was, about the year 365, murdered by his pupils with their styles, by order of the emperor Julian. And now I think we have talked enough about pens and ink.

Ernest. I am not weary, but I shall be glad to come to *books.*

Uncle. I have already told you that when you read in Scripture of *books,* you must not think of such volumes as we now have, made of hundreds of leaves of paper, stitched and pasted, and bound and gilt. Most of the ancient books were rolls. The skins, parchments, linen, cotton, silk, and even papyrus, were thus rolled.

Hilary. Were these rolls very large?

Uncle. Of various sizes, as are our books. Usually the roll was long, but narrow. When a very large book was needed, many skins were joined together. I have showed you a Jewish roll. I suppose the books of the Old Testament were on rolls of the same sort. When there was no room on one side for more, they used to write on the other. This explains a text in Ezekiel, (ii. 9 :) " And when I looked, behold a hand was sent unto me, and, lo, a *roll of a book* was therein ; and he *spread* it (unrolled it) before me ; and it was *written within and without.*"

Hilary. Did the Greeks and Romans use such rolls ?

Uncle. They did. In Herculaneum many such

have been found, and pictures of many more, which give you a better idea of ancient books than a talk of a whole day. By referring to an engraving under the article before mentioned, you will see how a book was held in reading. You will also see that the writing was sometimes *across* the roll; just as if you took a newspaper and held it by the sides. Thus the book is in *colamns* or *pages*, though there is but one *leaf*. In Jeremiah, (ch. xxxvi.) we read that Baruch, the prophet's friend, took down his words *with ink* in a *book* that is, a roll. In ver. 20 it is called a *roll*. Jehudi read it aloud to the king; and when " he had read two or three *leaves*," that is, such columns as you see in the cut, " the king cut it with a penknife, and cast it into the fire that was on the hearth, until the roll was consumed in the fire that was on the hearth." ver. 23. By another engraving under the same article, you will see another form of holding the books to read them. This roll is narrower than the other, and far narrower than the Jewish rolls.

Ernest. Did our Saviour read in the synagogue out of such books as this ?

Uncle. Rather out of such a roll as I showed you yesterday. When he came to the synagogue at Nazareth, " there was delivered to him the book of the prophet Esaias." This was the roll which contained Isaiah's prophecy. "And when he had *opened the book*," or more correctly, 'when he had *unrolled* the book,' that is, to find the proper column or page, he found the portion he sought. Having read it, "he *closed the book*,"—he rolled it up again, "and gave it again to the minister, and sat down," and began to preach. Luke iv. 16—20.

Hilary. I always imagined that the writing on these rolls was from one end to the other of the long roll.

Uncle. Some were certainly so. We have another figure from Herculaneum, which represents a nymph singing out of a book. You will see copied, under the same article in the DICTIONARY, the roll and the hands. You will see it was read down the roll. You can also see that it is poetry, and is divided into stanzas of six lines each.

Ernest. The Jewish roll which you showed us yesterday is different from these in one respect. It has rollers of wood like those on maps.

Uncle. Rollers are used in all the synagogue rolls, and the ends of these are often highly ornamented with silver or gold. The ancients had the same contrivance. The rod or cylinder was of ebony, cedar, cypress, box, bone, or ivory. The ornamental caps at the projecting ends of the rollers were called the *horns.*

Ernest. I cannot understand what is meant by the *seals* of books. How can a book be sealed ?

Uncle. This is soon explained. Suppose I take that Hebrew roll, and wind a cord or band round it, and put a little sealing-wax over the knot. The book is then *sealed.* And I may seal it six or seven times if I choose. Let me show you this in a little drawing. Now you see that such a book could not be opened without breaking the seal.

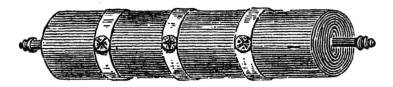

Hilary. And were letters sealed in the same way ?

Uncle. They often were ; of course the rolls were then smaller. Take the Bible, and turn to Isa. xxix. 11.

Hilary. " And the vision of all is become unto you as the words of a *book that is sealed,* which men deliver to one that is learned, saying, ' Read this, I pray thee ;' and he saith, ' I cannot, for it is sealed.' "

Uncle. Read Dan. xii. 4.

Hilary. " But thou, O Daniel, shut up the words, and *seal the book.*"

Uncle. Read Rev. v. 1, and vi. 1.

Hilary. " And I saw in the right hand of him that sat on the throne a *book,* written within and on the back side, *sealed with seven seals.*" " And I saw when the Lamb *opened one of the seals.*"

Uncle. The roll was *full,* inside and outside, and was fastened with seals which no one could open.

Ernest. But were all the ancient books in this form ?

Uncle. No. I have already told you that some of them, but more rarely, resembled ours. Here is another drawing from Herculaneum.

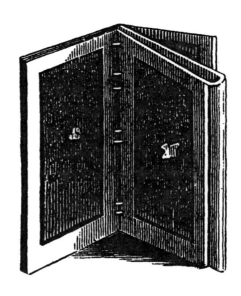

Ernest. I suppose they did not put rolls up on *shelves* as we do.

Uncle. No. They had various cases to keep them in. Some of these were more like pails or casks than book-cases. See here; this cut represents an ancient Roman *scrinium,* or book-case.

'The little *labels* at the top of the volumes contain the titles.

Ernest. Do you suppose the epistles of Paul and the other apostles were written on rolls?

Uncle. I have no doubt they were on rolls of papyrus or parchment. The ancients had scribes who wrote their letters. The person sending the letter, *dictated*, that is, told the secretary what to write. The Romans called such a scribe an *amanuensis*.

Ernest. Did not Paul write his epistles with his own hand?

Uncle. Not commonly. When he did so, he mentions it as remarkable. Thus he says to the Galatians : "Ye see how large a letter I have written unto you *with mine own hand.*" Gal. vi. 11.

Hilary. How did they know then that such letters were not forged?

Uncle. Paul always added his *name*, or some *salutation* in his own writing. "The salutation of Paul with mine own hand, which is the *token* in every epistle." 2 Thess. iii. 17. "The salutation of me Paul with mine own hand." 1 Cor. xvi. 21. And when he wrote a letter to the Romans, his secretary Tertius adds a kind salutation : "I, *Tertius, who wrote this epistle,* salute you in the Lord." Rom. xvi. 22. In the Old Testament, we find that Queen Jezebel "wrote letters in Ahab's name, and sealed them with his seal." 1 Kings xxi. 8. At the present day the letters of the orientals are oftener *tied* than *sealed ;* and their books are not commonly *rolled,* but made like ours. But when a letter is sent to a great man, it is bound in various costly envelopes, and sealed with great care.

All this I hope will give you a better idea of the books of Scripture than you had before. You perceive that when any one had the whole Bible, he had it often in a great number of little rolls. And many had only a few of these. Let us bless God that we have the whole, in a portable volume.

CHAPTER VIII.

Ancient Bibles—Of the copying of books—Ornamental writing
and illumination—Church bibles—Cost of ancient books—
Ornamented covers—Value of books in the middle ages—
Translations of the Bible—The Septuagint—The Vulgate—
Other versions—Into Anglo-Saxon—Into English—Wiclif's
New Testament—Tindal's Bible—Love of English Christians
for the Scriptures—The Bishop's Bible—Collections of trans-
lations.

EVERY day that Ernest and Hilary spent with
their affectionate uncle, they learned something
new concerning the Holy Scriptures. They were
so much gratified with his conversations, that they
no longer needed to be called, but went every morning into his study without an invitation. And he
was equally pleased to receive them, for he had no
greater pleasure than to communicate useful knowledge to his young relations.

When he saw them coming in the next day, he
began as follows :

I have already told you, my dear nephews, that
the books of the Bible were not all written at the
same time. The Old Testament books are supposed to have been collected and arranged by Ezra.
And after that time, they were preserved by the
Jews with the greatest care. They took all possi-

ble measures to keep them from being altered in a single letter. It was a long time before the New Testament books were collected in the same way. For many years they were circulating through different parts of the world, as separate volumes ; and there were comparatively few persons who possessed the whole Scriptures. At length the whole were gathered, and acknowledged by all the church as the genuine Scriptures.

Hilary. As they did not know how to print, I suppose every one had to copy off the whole book for himself.

Uncle. Some persons did so. But *copying* was a regular trade in those days, just as *printing* is now. And there were men who spent their whole lives in copying, and who could write with a beauty and regularity which are unknown at the present day.

Hilary. How long did this continue to be the case ?

Uncle. Until the invention of printing in the fifteenth century. Multitudes of monks in monasteries used to spend their lives in transcribing manuscripts. In the abbey of Marmoutier, the most ancient that now remains in France, the monks lived in separate cells. No art or business was permitted among them except that of writing. Fifty-eight volumes were copied in Glastonbury in England, during the government of one abbot, about A. D. 1300. This was the chief employment of the Carthusian monks.

Ernest. How long it must have taken to write off the whole Bible !

Uncle. It was tedious indeed ; and this made books exceedingly dear. Besides this, many of these ancient manuscripts were highly adorned. Some were written in letters of purple, silver, or gold. Some were ornamented with pictures around the principal capital letters, which were called *illuminations.* I have seen many thus embellished. There is in the Vienna library a copy of Genesis and of Luke, about fourteen hundred years old. It is on purple vellum, in letters of gold and silver.

Ernest. Were there Bibles in all the ancient churches ?

Uncle. There were ; at least until the Romish church forbade the reading of the Scriptures. Bibles were placed in convenient places, within the church walls, that the common people might come and read when they chose.

Ernest. This was very well when books were so expensive.

Uncle. The cost of books was greater than you would suppose. A single anecdote will show this. In the fourth century a monk named *Hilarion* went in a ship from Lybia to Sicily. When he arrived at his port, he offered to pay for his passage and that of his companion, with a copy of the *gospels* which he had written in his youth. The captain, seeing they had nothing else, allowed them to go free.

Sometimes the elegance of the cover or binding made them more costly. *Ina*, king of the West Saxons, gave to the church at Glastonbury, for the " coverings of the books of the gospels," twenty pounds and sixty pieces of gold. In 1430, an English abbot paid for the binding of a single book three pounds; and you must remember, that a pound at that time would buy four cows or three horses; so that he laid out the value of nine horses on the cover of his book! It is just as if I should give four or five hundred dollars for binding a volume. In the reign of Henry II. the sheriffs of London paid, by the king's order, twenty-two shillings for *gold to gild the gospel used in the king's chapel.*

Hilary. I feel glad that we live when books are cheaper.

Uncle. Yes, my son, we should be truly thankful that we are so favoured. In 609, Alfred, king of Northumberland, gave eight hundred acres of land for the History of the World. And the same man who paid three pounds for covering his book, paid five pounds for the copying of it. In the tenth century books were so scarce in Spain, that the same volumes used to serve for several monasteries. And a single copy of the Bible, and a few other books, not more than sixteen, were so important a legacy, that it was witnessed by the king, queen, and several bishops. Prayers used to be said, after the manner of that ignorant age, for the souls of such as had given books to a monastery. These books were most carefully kept, and when, as a great favour, they were lent, it was regularly certified in a legal writing.

Ernest. But did books continue to be so dear, even in England?

Uncle. Even after the Reformation began to dawn, books were scarce. *Wiclif's* Translation of the New Testament cost more than a poor man could pay. In 1424, a *Mass Book* was sold for *five marks*, (£3 6s. 8d.,) or nearly fifteen dollars, equal to the salary of a curate for a year. When printing was invented, nothing used to surprise the people so much as that a Bible could be bought for forty crowns. In 1521, when many poor people in Lincolnshire were burned by the papists, I read that one John Collins paid for a printed Bible *twenty shillings*, or less than five dollars; being then as much as the wages of a master carpenter for forty days, or the price of four hundred and eighty pounds of beef.

As I said before, you see how thankful we ought to be that we live at a time, and in a country, where every one can have the sacred Scriptures, and especially that we can have them translated into our own language.

Ernest. I should like to hear something about the *translations* of the Bible.

Uncle. The earliest translation of which we have any certain account, is what is called the *Septuagint.* It is so called because it was made by about seventy Jews, and *septuaginta* is the Latin for seventy. It was in *Greek*, and was made by order of *Ptolemy Philadelphus*, king of Egypt, who was a great collector of books. This was made about two hundred and fifty years before Christ. It was this version which was used by the early Christians.

Hilary. Was not the Bible translated into Latin?

Uncle. It was ; several times. The only Latin version, however, which I think necessary to mention, is the *Vulgate,* which is considered the standard by the Romish church. The word *vulgate* means *common.* It was made towards the close of the fourth century, by *Jerome,* a celebrated father of the church.

Ernest. Was the Bible translated into many other languages ?

Uncle. Yes, it was natural for this to happen. Whenever Christianity came into a new country, the people would wish to have the Bible in their mother tongue. The wicked and impious practice of withholding the Scriptures from the people had not yet begun. Pious missionaries laboured to multiply translations, and many of these are still in existence.

Hilary. Were there any translations into *English?*

Uncle. You must know that the English language is formed out of one called the *Anglo-Saxon*, or *Saxon*, which was spoken in England some centuries ago. The first translation of which I have read was by *Adhelm*, Bishop of Sherborne, about the year 706. He translated the Psalms into Saxon. The four gospels were translated by *Egbert*, another bishop, who died A. D. 721. The whole Bible was translated by the venerable *Bede*, a few years after. About two hundred years later, King *Alfred* made a new translation of the Psalms. And *Elfric*, Archbishop of Canterbury, about A. D. 995, translated a large portion of the Bible.

Ernest. You say these were *Saxon ;* but when was the first *English* translation made ?

Uncle. About A. D. 1290, by an unknown author. Towards the end of the fourteenth century, that is about 1380, the great JOHN WICLIF, who is some-

times called the " Morning-star of the Reformation," translated the whole New Testament into
English. This was very offensive to the papists,
and some persons endeavoured to get it suppressed
by the parliament, but without success. But for
a long time afterwards, many thousands were persecuted and slain for reading this book.

Hilary. Was the English of those people the
same which we speak now?

Uncle. Let me give you a specimen. I will
let you read several verses out of *Wiclif's* New
Testament, which I have here:

Now my soule is troublid, and what
schal I seye, fadir, saue me fro this our:
but therefor I cam into this our. Fadir,
clarifie thi name. And a vois cam fro
heuene and seide, and I haue clarified,
and eft I schal clarifie. (John xii. 27, 28.)

For in alle thynges ghe ben maad riche
in him in ech word and in ech kunnyng
as the witnessyng of Crist is confirmed
in ghou, so that no thyng fail in ghou in
ony grace that abiden the schewing of
our Lord Jhesus Crist. (1 Cor. i. 5—7.)

I do thankyngis to my God in alle
mynde of ghou euermore in all my
preieris for ghou alle with ioie, and make

a bisechïng on ghoure compnyng in this gospel of Crist fro the firste date til now. (Phil. i. 4, 5.)

I comaunde to thee before God that quickeneth alle thyngis and bifore Crist Jesu that gheldïde a witnessyng undir Pilat of Pounce a good confessïoun, that thou kepe the comaundment without wemme without repreef into the comyng of oure Lord Jesu Crist, whom the blessïd and aloone myghti Kyng of kyngis, and Lord of lordïs schal schew in his tymes. (1 Tim. vi. 13—15.)

Hilary. O, I can scarcely understand a word of it.

Ernest. When was the first English Bible *printed?*

Uncle. The first Bible printed was the translation by *William Tindal.* He went to Antwerp in Flanders, and there finished his translation of the whole Bible. He was assisted by *John Fry,* or *Fryth,* and *William Joy;* the former of whom was burned at the stake by the papists in 1533, and the latter suffered in the same way in Portugal. The first edition of the New Testament was bought up by the popish bishop of London, and burned. But with the money paid for this, others were printed. Those who were suspected of importing these books into England, were condemned, by Sir Thomas More, to ride with their faces to the tails of their horses, and to throw the books publicly into a fire. Many thousands were, however, circulated. Multitudes learned to read. Many used to travel far, and sit up all night in barns or sheds, hearing the word read, and thus committing it to memory. Tindal himself suffered martyrdom in 1536, near Brussels, having been seized by order of King Henry VIII. He died praying, " *Lord, open the King of England's eyes.*"

Ernest. You have given us a specimen of *Wiclif's* translation: will you please to give us a specimen of *Tindal's ?*

Uncle. With pleasure. You must remember that, in that day, books were printed in what is called *Black Letter* or *Old English.* Here it is.

Matthew, chap. v.

Ye haue herde, how it is sayde: thou shalt loue thyne neghboure, and hate thine enemy. But I saye unto you: loue youre enemies; Blesse them that curse you; Do good to them that hate you; Praye for them which do you wrong and persecute you, that ye may be the children of youre father which is in heaven; for he maketh his sonne to aryse on the euel and on the good, and sendeth his rayne on the just and unjust. For yf ye loue them which loue you, what rewarde shall ye haue? Do not the Publicans euen so?

This was an excellent translation. In many parts of it, Tindal was helped by *Miles Coverdale* The whole Bible, when it was published in **1535,** was dedicated to the pious young King Edward VI., who was a friend to the Reformation. It was the first English Bible issued by royal authority. It was ordered that one of them should be in every church. *John Rogers*, the first martyr in Queen Mary's reign, was apprehended for having been concerned in this publication.

Hilary. I dare say the good Protestants were glad to have this book.

Uncle. They were so, indeed, as you will see by an anecdote which I will tell you.*

It was wonderful, says a historian, to see with what joy this book was received, not only among the more learned sort, but all over England, among all the common people. Everybody who was able bought the book, or busily read it, or got others to read it aloud. Many elderly people

---

* Strype, Mem. I. b. i. c. 17.

learned to read on purpose. Even little boys flocked among the rest to hear portions read.

There was a lad named *William Maldon* who lived at Chelmsford, in Essex. Several poor men of this town bought the New Testament, and on Sundays they used to sit and read it at the lower end of the church. Many people used to collect to hear, and among the rest, William, who was then fifteen years old. His father took notice of this, and one day came in a passion, and took him away, to say his Latin prayers. This grieved him very much. As often as he used to return to hear the reading, his father used to take him away. This made him desire to learn to read for himself; and he succeeded. He and an apprentice of his father's laid their money together, and bought a New Testament. They hid it under the bed-straw. One night, while his father was asleep, he and his mother were talking about worshipping the crucifix, and William said it was idolatry. His mother informed upon him, and his father flew into a rage, arose from his bed, pulled William by the hair of his head, and whipped him unmercifully. Many years after, William told good Mr. Fox, that he bore this beating without a tear, and even with joy, because it was for Christ's sake. This enraged his father still more, so that he ran down and brought a halter, and put it round his neck, threat-

ening to hang him. At length, by his mother's en-
treaties, the cruel father ceased, leaving him almost
dead. There are many such anecdotes in a book
called "*Fox's* Acts and Monuments." I could
tell you of several other translations and editions,
but none of them are so important as the *Bishops'
Bible.*

Ernest. When was this printed?

Uncle. In 1568. It was proposed by Archbishop Parker, and by authority of the crown.
He divided the whole Bible into fifteen portions,
and gave these to fifteen learned men, for each of
them to translate his part. It was furnished with
maps, plates, and some notes.

Ernest. Why was it called the Bishops' Bible?

Uncle. Because eight of the fifteen learned men
who translated it were *bishops.* In 1571, it was
ordered that one of these should be in every church.

Hilary. If there were as many translations of
the Bible in other countries as there were in England, they would make a large library of themselves.

Uncle. Some persons have endeavoured to
make such a collection. In 1768, Charles, Duke
of Wurtemburg, began a great library, and among
other things, he collected all the different editions
of the Bible he could find, in every language. The
whole number of Bibles, in 1804, was *nine thou-*

sand, and he still wanted three thousand more to complete the collection.

But, my dear boys, I must not keep you here any longer, for it is time that you were at your exercises out of doors. To-morrow I am to give you the history of the English Bible which we now use.

CHAPTER IX.

The authorized English version—Extent of its influence—History—King James the First—Authors of this translation—Occasion of their undertaking the work—Account of its progress—Manner of dividing the labour—Their great care in comparing and correcting—The learning of these translators—Revision of the whole—Printing of the English Bible—List of translators' names.

I HAVE said that uncle Austin had a great collection of valuable books. Among them, there were several ancient English Bibles. One of these, a folio volume, lay upon his table when the boys entered for their morning entertainment. As the old gentleman saw his nephews coming, he laid his finger on the book, and said :

"Here, my boys, is the best translation ever made of the Bible."

Hilary. Which is that, dear uncle ?

Uncle. It is our common English Bible, but it goes by various names. Sometimes it is called simply, *The English Version*, because it is the latest and best of the Bibles in our language. Sometimes it is called *The authorized Version*, because it was published by the authority of the government, and because the use of it is enjoined by many churches. Sometimes it is called *King James's Version*, because it was made by his order. We may also call it the *Common Version* or *Translation*. And whatever we call it, we must acknowledge that it is one of the greatest blessings which God has ever conferred on any land or nation.

Ernest. It seems to me, uncle, as if it was given to a great many lands and nations.

Hilary. How so, Ernest?

Ernest. Because it is in *English*, and English is spoken in many different countries.

Uncle. You are right, Ernest, and your expression is more just than mine. The English Version is a gift of God to many millions. If none were to read it but the inhabitants of the single island of Great Britain, it would be a great thing; for there are, in that island alone, more than sixteen millions of souls. Then there are more than seven millions in Ireland. So you see there are more than twenty-four millions of people in these two islands; and among all of these the Bible may be carried, but we must add many more.

Ernest. Yes, because here in America we all talk English.

Hilary. Not *all*, for there are a good many Germans, and Frenchmen, and Spaniards.

Uncle. Ernest's remark is true in the general.

In the United States, there is not one in a thousand who does not understand English. Now what is the population of the United States?

Ernest and Hilary. More than twelve millions.

Uncle. Then you must add, all the people in the East and West Indies who speak English, and all those in British America, and the south of Africa. Every day we live, our language is gaining ground in the world, and it seems plain that Providence has ordered this to be so, that the saving knowledge which abounds in English books might be spread all over the world. But now for the book itself. Look here, and read this title-page.

Ernest. The spelling looks old-fashioned, but I believe I can read it.

" *The Holy Bible, conteyning the Old Testament and the New, newly translated out of the Originall Tongues, and with the former Translations diligently compared and revised by his Majesties special Comandment. Imprinted at London, by Robert Barker, Printer to the King's most excellent Majestie. 1611.*"

Hilary. Pray what is that mark over the *m* in the word *commandment?*

Uncle. I think you might guess; it is to make up for one of the *m*'s which is left out. It was used by the old scriveners to save room, and is very common in ancient Latin books.

Hilary. What is meant by the *King's most excellent majesty?*

Uncle. It is a common term in monarchies for the monarch himself : here it means King James I. What do you know about him ?

Ernest. He was the first of the house of Stuart that reigned in England. The Scottish and English crowns were united in him. He came to the English throne in 1603, and died in 1625. He was the son of Mary, Queen of Scots.

Hilary. James I. was a weak man, but had a great deal of knowledge. He was always trying to show his learning. He was also disposed to be a tyrant. We have learned a great deal more about him at school.

Uncle. That is sufficient. You may now see the advantage of knowing a little history. What you say of James is true ; yet, after all, he did some very good things ; and the best of these was the version before your eyes.

Ernest. But, sir, did the king make it himself?

Uncle. Not exactly, but he caused it to be done. And I am now about to tell you the way in which this came about. When James ascended the throne, he found there were great disputes and differences among his new subjects about church government and doctrines. Most of the people were fond of episcopacy, but some who were called Puritans, were opposed to it   These Puritans begged the king to allow a conference, or meeting, at which the chief men of the two sides might argue the matter in a friendly way.   He consented to this, and appointed a conference, which took place at Hampton Court, in 1604. The king presided as moderator.   Dr. John Reynolds, or Reynolds, was the chief speaker of the Puritans, and petitioned for a new translation of the Bible.   He gave some instances to show that the previous translations were faulty.

Ernest. What did the king say to this ?

Uncle. He agreed that there ought to be a new version, made by the most learned men, which should be used by every one : because there was great confusion arising from the variety of Bibles in use.   And accordingly, in 1604, he appointed fifty-four learned men, and commanded them to set about the work of making a new translation.

Ernest. Did they all come together to do it ?

Uncle. No.   Indeed only forty-seven actually went through with the work.   The other seven either declined the task, or were removed by death.   These forty-seven were distributed among three cities, *Westminster*, *Oxford*, and *Cambridge.*

Ernest. Is Westminster a *city?*

Uncle. It is ; though it is now considered as

a part of London. Taken together with South-wark, they make up the great metropolis of Great Britain. You know that the other two cities are those in which the two famous universities are. It was very natural to suppose that the greatest number of learned men would be in these three places. But I was about to answer Ernest's question, thus: The translators were divided into *six* sets or classes. These sets were called *companies*.

Ernest. That makes just two for each of the three places.

Uncle. It does. There were two companies at Westminster, two at Cambridge, and two at Oxford. Of the translators, seventeen were at Westminster, fifteen at Cambridge, and fifteen at Oxford. Each company worked by itself, and each had a particular part of the work assigned to it. You must remember that they included the *apocryphal books*.

Ernest. I should like to understand how they managed this difficult business.

Uncle. I will try to make it clear to you. Remember there were six companies, and in each company seven or eight individuals. Now let us take a single company, and see how it proceeded. We will say, for example, the first of the Oxford companies. This contained seven individuals. To this company were assigned the major and minor

prophets.   Now each of these seven persons studied his portion at home by himself.   Then he
wrote the best translation he could of certain chapters agreed upon.   Then, on a certain day, all the
seven met together, each one bringing the translation he had made.   Here they compared their versions, discussed difficulties, and talked the matter
over, until they had agreed on some translation.
When they had got through with all the prophets,
they had their work transcribed, and sent a copy
to each of the other five companies.

Ernest. But what if their translation did not
please the other companies ?

Uncle. This must have happened frequently,
and provision was made by the king for such dis-
agreement.   As soon as a version was brought to
a company for examination, all the members met.
One read the new translation, and each of the
others held in his hand some Bible, in Hebrew,
Greek, French, Italian, &c.   If no one said any
thing, the translation was accepted.   But when any
one was dissatisfied, he spoke out and mentioned
it.   If the company thought the translation wrong,
they marked the error, and sent back an account of
it to those who had made the version.   And it was
changed or not, according to the final judgment of
the whole.

Hilary. Was there ever any general meeting of the whole forty-seven ?

Uncle. I am unable to discover whether *all* of them ever convened. The king's rule however was, that differences were to be settled " at the *general meeting*, which is to be of the *chief persons* of each company, at the end of the work."*

There was another rule, that in very difficult questions, they might get the help of any other learned men. And every bishop in England was commanded to inform all his clergy that the Bible was translating, and to request the use of such critical notes as any of them might have made.

Ernest. Surely the version ought to be good, for I cannot think how a better method could have been used.

Uncle. The plan was wise, and the result is blessed.

Ernest. I have heard people say that our translation was made in an ignorant age.

Uncle. If they meant that it was made by ignorant men, they spoke either falsely or ignorantly. I suppose there were never united in any one literary labour, an equal number of men, possessing an equal amount of learning. True, there are some

---

* Rule 10. See these rules in Todd's Vindication, 9—12 Horne, iii. 248.

things better understood in our day, but there were also scholars in that day far superior to most now living.*   Thirteen of the number were heads (or presidents) of colleges. Six were bishops. Among these was Abbot, afterwards Archbishop of Canterbury. A number of them were selected for their wonderful knowledge of the oriental languages. One of them, *Dr. Layfield*, was chosen on account of his great skill in architecture, and his judgment was much relied upon in what relates to the tabernacle and temple. *Master Edward Lively*, as he was called, was the greatest orientalist among them, but he died before the work was done.

Ernest. How long did it take them to make this version ?

Uncle. It was begun in 1607, and it was completed in 1610. It took them, therefore, almost three years. When the whole was finished, three copies were sent to London ; that is, one copy from each of the three cities.

Hilary. Then, I suppose, the king had it printed immediately.

Uncle. Not immediately. His plan was too wise to allow him to hurry matters. Six men were appointed to revise the whole, two from the

---

* See the lives of these eminently learned men in Townley's Illustrations, iii. p. 290, seq.

joint-company of each city. They met daily in the Stationers' Hall, London. They finished their part of the work in nine months. And to conclude, the whole was finally revised by *Dr. Smith*, afterwards Bishop of Gloucester. It is he who wrote the preface found in the old editions.*

Ernest. I cannot help feeling a great respect for this old volume. According to what you say, this was printed the very year after the work was done.

Uncle. It was. There are copies which have on the title-page, 1612 and 1613.

Hilary. It must have been received with great joy by all the pious people in England.

Uncle. It was indeed a joyful day; yet not so much so as when the other translations appeared; for the people had several versions already, especially the *Bishops' Bible.* And whatever faults there may have been in these, they were, in the main, correct. You have heard it said, with truth, that the very worst translation contains enough to save the soul.

The Bishops' Bible was a great blessing. It ought not to be forgotten. The work of these great translators would have been immensely more difficult, if they had not possessed such a previous version. And the very first rule which King

---

* It may be seen in Bagster's Comprehensive Bible.

James laid down for them, was, that the Bishops' Bible was to be followed, and altered as little as the original would permit. This is the reason why many of the proper names are strangely written.

Hilary. My mother has a Prayer Book, such as is used in the church of England; and the *Psalms of David* in it are very different from what they are in our Bibles.

Uncle. True. When our authorized version was published, the Prayer Book had been already compiled. The *Psalms*, and the *Epistles* and *Gospels* in the Common Prayer were from old versions. The Epistles and Gospels were from the Bishops' Bible; but in 1661, they were exchanged for the new version. But the *Psalms* were according to the translation of Cranmer's Bible, and so they remain to this day. But however the translators may have been indebted to those who preceded them, they have laid the church of Christ under a special obligation. As old Fuller says: "These, with Jacob, rolled away the stone from the mouth of the well of life; so that now even Rachel's weak women may freely come, both to drink themselves, and water the flocks of their families at the same."*

Ernest. I should be obliged to you, uncle, if

---

* Fuller's Church History, c. x. p. 68.

you would give me, on a piece of paper, the names of these translators.

Uncle. With pleasure. The thought is a good one. You may then find out at your leisure who they all were. Wait a few minutes, and I will copy them out of good old Fuller. And you shall have them in their companies, and the parts which they translated.

I. THE FIRST WESTMINSTER COMPANY. 10.

Dr. Lancelot Andrews,
Dr. John Overall,
Dr. Adrian à Saravia,
Dr. John Layfield,
Dr. Tighe,*
Mr. Burleigh,
Mr. King,
Mr. Thompson,
Mr. Bedwell.

The five books of Moses, and onward through second Kings.

II. THE FIRST CAMBRIDGE COMPANY. 8.

Mr. Edward Lively,
Dr. Richardson,
Dr. Chaderton,
Mr. Dillingham,
Mr. Harrison,
Mr. Andrews,
Mr. Spalding,
Mr. Bing.

The remaining historical books, with Job, Psalms, Proverbs, Canticles, and Ecclesiastes.

---

* Not *Leigh,* as in some lists.

III. THE FIRST OXFORD COMPANY. 7.

Dr. Harding,
Dr. Reynolds,
Dr. Holland,
Dr. Kilby,
Dr. Miles Smith,
Mr. Brett,
Mr. Fairclome.

The Prophets, and the Lamentations of Jeremiah.

IV. THE SECOND CAMBRIDGE COMPANY. 7.

Dr. Duport,
Dr. Branthhwait
Dr. Radcliffe,
Mr. Ward, (of Emanuel College,)
Mr. Ward, (of King's College,)
Mr. Downes,
Mr. Boyse.

The Prayer of Manasses, and rest of Apocrypha.

V. THE SECOND OXFORD COMPANY. 8.

Dr. Thomas Ravis,
Dr. George Abbot,
Dr. Edes,
Dr. Giles Thompson,
Mr. Saville,
Dr. Peryn,
Dr. Ravens,
Mr. John Harmar.

The Gospels, Acts, and Revelation.

VI. THE SECOND WESTMINSTER COMPANY. 7.

Dr. William Barlow,
Dr. Hutchinson,
Dr. Spencer,
Mr. Fenton,   } The Epistles.
Mr. Rabbett,
Mr. Sanderson,
Mr. Dakins.

CHAPTER X.

Names of Scripture books—Double names—Apocalypse—Books
of Samuel and Kings—The Preacher—Canticles—Divisions
of the Bible continued—Lesser divisions—Chapters, paragraphs, and verses—History of the division into chapters—
Jewish divisions—Concordances—Sancto Caro—History of
the division into verses—Henry Stephens—Advantages and
disadvantages of these divisions.

THE day after that in which uncle Austin gave
his account of the English Bible was exceedingly
cold. There had been a great snow during the
night, and the strong wind had blown it into high
banks, so that in many places the fences were entirely covered up. This made the good old gentleman feel some anxiety about his sheep, lest some
of them should have been buried in the snow-drifts;
a thing which often happens in hard winters. He
therefore went out, immediately after breakfast, to
attend to the poor animals, remembering the words of
Scripture, *A righteous man regardeth the life of his
beast*.* This employed him for more than an hour,
and during his absence the boys amused themselves
with the various books and maps which lay upon
his table. When uncle Austin came in again, he

---

* Prov. xii. 10.

found Ernest and Hilary engaged in a little debate about the meaning of a word which they had met with in their reading. It was the word *Apocalypse*.

Uncle. O, my boys, the word *Apocalypse* is only another name for the last book in the Bible. *Apocalypse* is the Greek for *Revelation*.

Hilary. Why, sir, have any of the books more than one name?

Uncle. Yes, my son, there are several variations of this kind. In different languages, of course, the names differ very much : and even in our own language we often call the same book by two names. Just turn over the leaves of that large Oxford Bible ; look at the titles of the several books, and I think you will discover what I mean.

Ernest. Yes. I think I have already found a place of the sort you mean. *The First Book of Samuel, otherwise called The First Book of the Kings.*

Uncle. Exactly so. You will find the same thing in the second book of Samuel. And if you look farther, at the beginning of what we commonly call *First Kings*, you will see a similar difference.

Ernest. I do. *The First Book of the Kings, commonly called The Third Book of the Kings.*

Hilary. Yes ; but, uncle, it seems to me that this book is *not* commonly called *The Third Book of the Kings*. Do we not commonly say *First Sa-*

muel—Second Samuel—and then *First Kings —. Second Kings ?*

Uncle. We do so now-a-days. But two hundred years ago, when our translation was first used, everybody counted *four books* of Kings, and this was the *third.* I will tell you the reason of this. You remember I spoke to you of the famous Latin translation, called the *Vulgate.** This was used, and is to this day used, among Roman Catholics. After the Reformation, the same names of the books which people had learned from the Vulgate were very naturally used ; making a little alteration in the Latin names, so as to change them into English. In this way we borrow from the Latin the very names which they borrowed from the Greek.

Hilary. I have found another double title—*Ecclesiastes, or the Preacher.*

Uncle. Yes, that is a good instance. The Hebrew name of this book of Solomon is KOHELETH. This word means *The Preacher.* The Greeks turned it into *Ecclesiastes,* which means the same thing. The Latins borrowed this from the Greek, and the English borrowed it from the Latin.

Ernest. Are any more of the books known by two names ?

---

* See p. 99.

Uncle. Yes, the very next book, which is *The Song of Solomon*, is often called the *Canticles.*

Ernest. Is *Canticles* also a Greek word ?

Uncle. No. It is an English word, derived from the Latin. In the Vulgate this book is called *Canticum Canticorum*, or the *Song of Songs.* Read the first verse of it in that Bible, and you will find the very expression. From all this you will see that the names of the various books have often been changed. At the present time, the Germans, instead of saying *Genesis, Exodus.* &c., say *First Book of Moses, Second Book of Moses*, &c. But I think we have now been long enough upon the names, for I wish to go to something more interesting.

Ernest. There is one question I should like to ask before you go any further. Are the books of Scripture always arranged in the same order ?

Uncle. Not exactly. The Hebrew differs from the Greek. And in our version we chiefly follow the arrangement of the Septuagint, or Greek translation. In the Hebrew Bible, the books are arranged like ours as far as second Kings. Then come the whole of the Prophets, except Daniel, and the remaining books follow in this order : Psalms, Proverbs, Job, Song of Solomon, Ruth, Lamentations, Ecclesiastes, Esther, *Daniel*, Ezra, Nehemiah, Chronicles.

I wish now to speak to you of the *divisions* of the Bible. And let me ask you this question. *Into how many different parts or portions is the Bible divided ?* Ernest, lay that large Bible before you, and give me an answer.

Ernest. That is easily answered. The Bible is divided into two great portions—the *Old Testament* and the *New Testament.*

Uncle. Very well. Now tell me some smaller division.

Ernest. Each Testament is divided into *books.*

Uncle. Very well, again. Here we have a second division, into *books.* Go on.

Ernest. Each book is divided into *chapters.*

Hilary. Wait a moment, brother. Some of the little books are not divided into chapters at all.

Uncle. I am pleased to see you on the alert. There are some books, such as *Obadiah, Philemon,* second and third epistles of *John,* and the epistle of *Jude,* which are not broken into chapters. Still it is correct to say in a general way that each book is divided into *chapters.* Proceed, Ernest.

Ernest. Each chapter is divided into *verses.* And this is the smallest division of all.

Uncle. True. But you have not observed a division which comes between the chapters and the verses.

Ernest. I cannot imagine what that is. I see no other division.

Hilary. Nor do I.

Uncle. Open your Bible again. Look at the first chapter of Genesis. After the number which marks the sixth verse, do you not observe a mark like an inverted P ?

Ernest. O yes, sir ! That is called a *paragraph*

Uncle. Very true. And this mark (¶) denotes the beginning of a new paragraph or small section. These sections are smaller than *chapters*, and commonly larger than *verses ;* yet sometimes the paragraph contains only a single verse, as in 1 Sam. xxiii. 29; unless we reckon this paragraph to end with verse 8 of the following chapter.

Ernest. What is the meaning of the word?

Uncle. The word *paragraph* is from the Greek, and means "a distinct part of a discourse." In common books a paragraph contains a number of sentences, and the blank space between paragraphs is much greater than between sentences. Commonly wherever there is a break in a line, it shows that a new paragraph is begun. But the Bible is so printed that there is just such a break, or blank space, between the verses. And therefore, in order to show where a new paragraph begins, this mark (¶) is put after the number of the verse.

Hilary. What is the use of this division into sections or paragraphs ?

Uncle. It shows that the writer is now going to another part of the subject. Let me explain this by the first chapter in the Bible. This chapter consists of seven paragraphs. The first contains five verses. The second contains three verses, viz. verses 6, 7, and 8. The third contains five verses, viz. 9, 10, 11, 12, and 13. The fourth, ten verses, viz. 14—23. And so on, to the end. Each of these little divisions treats of a different branch of the history. Thus the first is a general introduction. The second tells us of the creation of *light ;* the third, of the creation of the *firmament ;* and so on.

Ernest. Suppose we begin with the different sorts of divisions, and learn about them in regular order.

Uncle. Very well. But let me hear whether you can name them.

Ernest. The Bible is divided into, 1..Testaments ; 2. Books ; 3. Chapters ; 4. Paragraphs ; 5. Verses.

Uncle. We have already talked about the first two of these divisions, into Testaments and books. We will now proceed to the third, which is *chapters.*

Ernest. Was the Bible divided into these same chapters, when it was first written ?

Uncle. Not at all. The penmen of the several

books wrote *straight forward;* and, I suppose, made no division, except into sentences; unless when they came to the end of a sheet or leaf. In very ancient manuscripts there is no division even between the words.

Ernest. When was this division into chapters made?

Uncle. With the exception of the *Psalms,* which were always distinct, there was for some ages no division into these smaller portions. The five books of Moses were, indeed, parcelled into fifty or fifty-four large sections, called in Hebrew, *Parashioth.* One of these was read every Sabbath in the synagogue. And when, during the persecuted state of the Jews, they were forbidden to read the Pentateuch, they substituted the Prophets, which in like manner they parcelled into fifty-four larger sections, called in Hebrew, *Haphtoroth.* One of these was read every Sabbath. Each of these larger sections was also subdivided, but these portions did not correspond with the present chapters and verses.

Our present division into chapters was made by a learned theologian, named Hugo de Sancto Caro. He was a cardinal, which is the highest dignity below the pope, and lived about the middle of the thirteenth century, that is nearly six hundred years ago. Among his other labours, he undertook to make a concordance for the Latin Bible.

Hilary. What is a *concordance*?

Uncle. A concordance is a dictionary, by means of which we may find any passage of Scripture of which we remember a few words. For instance, I remember that there is a text which says that God "is able to abase" the proud. But I wish to have the exact words, and yet cannot recall the chapter and verse. I take this concordance, and look for the word *abase.* I read all the texts which contain this word. The fourth of them is the one I want. It is in the fourth chapter of Daniel, and the thirty-seventh verse : "Those that walk in pride he is able to abase." You perceive that such a book must be very useful. Now Sancto Caro, as I said, undertook to make such a concordance. But in order to be of any use, it must of course refer to the texts by means of some numbers. And as there were no numbered divisions, he divided the whole Bible into chapters, the same which we now have.

Hilary. Did he divide these again into verses ?

Uncle. Not exactly. He subdivided the chapters into smaller sections, somewhat larger than our present verses ; but instead of the numerals 1, 2, 3, 4, &c., he marked these smaller sections by the Roman letters A, B, C, D, E, F, and G, which were placed along the margin, at equal distances. Rabbi Nathan, a Jew, afterwards adopted the same chapters in the Hebrew Bible. Then they came into use in other languages, and were adopted in all the English versions of the Bible.

Ernest. Then I suppose the chapters are the same in all languages into which the Scriptures have been translated.

Uncle. Not altogether so. The chapters are divided differently in the Latin, the German, and the English; but this variation occurs only in a few cases.

Ernest. Now, sir, will you inform us when the division into verses took place?

Uncle. The Old and the New Testaments were not divided into verses at the same time. The Old Testament was thus divided by Athias, a Jew of Amsterdam, who introduced verses into an edition of the Hebrew Bible, which he printed in 1661. These same divisions were afterwards employed in other languages. The New Testament was thus divided by a celebrated publisher of ancient works, named Robert Stephens. We have an account of this from the pen of his son, Henry Stephens, who was also a famous scholar. I will read you his words. Henry Stephens says that there are two very remarkable circumstances relating to his father's division of the New Testament into verses. "The first is, that my father finished this division of each chapter into verses, while travelling from Paris to Lyons; and indeed the greater part of it, while riding by the way. The second fact is, that a short time prior to this journey, while he had the matter still in contemplation, almost all to whom he mentioned it, told him plainly, that he was an indiscreet man; as if he had wished to employ himself on an affair which would prove utterly useless. But behold the result : in opposition to the opinion which condemned and discountenanced my father's undertaking, as soon as his invention was published, every edition of the New Testament, whether in Greek, Latin, French, German, or in any other language, which did not adopt it, was immediately discarded."

Ernest. I can easily see what a great convenience it is, to have these divisions, great and small, and all numbered in regular order. If it were not for this, it would be very hard to point out where any particular text is found.

Uncle. True ; this is a great convenience, and thus an advantage to Bible-readers. Yet this seems to be the *only* advantage arising from this division ; and there are some great disadvantages.

Ernest. Pray tell me what they are, for I cannot think of any.

Uncle. In the first place, the divisions are sometimes injudicious and unhappy. Sentences are separated, which ought to have been left in connexion ; and a single sentence is sometimes broken into two or more verses. This very seriously affects the sense in certain places. Almost every reader, when he comes to the end of a verse, naturally supposes that the period is concluded—suspends his voice—and makes a full stop. Let me give you one or two instances. Hilary, turn to Colossians iv. 1. That verse, as you will see in a moment, ought to have ended the preceding chapter, being merely the close of the apostle's exhortation to masters and servants. Again, look at Psalm xcv. 7: *To-day if you will hear his voice,* (here the verse ends,) *harden not your hearts.* You perceive the sentence is broken in the very midst, where there is only a comma.——Read aloud the 12th verse of the next psalm.

Hilary. Let the field be joyful, and all that is therein ; then shall all the trees of the wood rejoice—

Uncle. See ! you have let your voice fall; yet the sentence goes on in the 13th verse. There is not even a comma: *Then shall all the trees of the wood rejoice before the Lord* ; yet the verses are divided between the words "rejoice" and "before."

In like manner the division into chapters often breaks the sense. The 53d chapter of Isaiah ("Who hath believed our report," &c.) cannot be understood, unless you begin with the 14th verse of

the preceding chapter. Look at that verse; it should
be the beginning of a chapter.

The verse 1 Cor. xii. 31, really is the introduction to the beautiful chapter which follows. Just
listen how close the connexion is. *But covet
earnestly the best gifts. And yet I show unto
you a more excellent way. Though I speak with
the tongues of men and of angels,* &c. If you
look at the twenty-first chapter of the Acts of the
Apostles, you will see that it ends in the middle of
a sentence, with only a comma. These instances
are enough to show you, that there are some disadvantages arising from an unhappy division.

Ernest. But suppose these few places were
divided more judiciously, would there still be any
evils in the division into chapters and verses?

Uncle. I think there would still be a disadvan-
tage, arising from the constant interruption of the
sense, by these small divisions. They break up
the whole narrative or discourse into a sort of dis-
jointed fragments. You would at once be sensible
of this, if I were to give you any other book divided
in this manner. Let us make the experiment.
Here is a sheet of paper on which I have copied a
part of the Pilgrim's Progress, divided into verses,
after the manner of our modern Bibles. I wish to
know what you think of it.

1. Now there was, not far from the place where they lay, a castle, called Doubting Castle, the owner whereof was Giant Despair ;

2. And it was in his grounds they were now sleeping.

3. Wherefore he getting up in the morning early, and walking up and down in his fields, caught Christian and Hopeful asleep in his grounds.

4. Then with a grim and surly voice, he bid them awake, and asked them whence they were, and what they did in his grounds.

5. They told him they were pilgrims, and that they had lost their way.

6. Then said the giant, You have this night trespassed on me, by trampling in, and lying on my grounds,

7. And therefore you must go along with me.

8. So they were forced to go, because he was stronger than they.

9. They also had but little to say, for they knew themselves in a fault.

10. The giant therefore drove them before him, and put them into his castle, in a very dark dungeon.

Hilary. O, I now see what you mean! These little divisions produce a constant stoppage—each sentence seems a thing by itself. I should soon grow weary of reading a book divided in this way.

Uncle. Exactly so; and for this very reason many persons grow more weary of reading the Scriptures, than they would otherwise be.

Ernest. But why does not some one print an edition of our English Bible just as other books are printed?

Uncle. O there have been several such. Look in the book-case behind you, and reach me the volumes in red morocco. This is just such an edition as you speak of. All these Bibles are undivided, except into ordinary paragraphs. But they have the number of the verse marked in the margin.

And now I think we may dismiss this subject for this morning.

CHAPTER XI.

Acroetics in the Bible—Running titles—Titles of the chapters—
The margin—Marginal notes—Divisions of these—Marginal
explanations — Marginal readings — Marginal references —
Two kinds of marginal readings—Use of these.

ERNEST and Hilary found that the conversation
of their uncle had this good effect, that it led them
to read more in the Scriptures than they had ever
done before. Often during the day, they might be
seen with their little pocket Bibles in their hands,
turning over the leaves, finding the places which
had been pointed out to them, and examining one
another upon what they had learned. The next
day was Sunday, and they spent much of their
time in careful reading of the Scriptures. On
Monday morning they hastened at a very early
hour to the study, where they found their affectionate uncle ready to receive them. "Well, my boys,"
said he, as he placed seats for them near the fire,
" what have you got to inquire about this morning ?"

Ernest. I think you said, sir, that the Psalms
were always divided just as they are at present.

Uncle. Yes. Because each psalm was a separate composition ; being a hymn or a prayer com-

posed on some special occasion.   They were afterwards collected and arranged as we now have
them.

Ernest. I have been looking at the 119th Psalm,
which seems to be the longest chapter in the Bible,
for it has a hundred and seventy-six verses.   But
I see that it is also divided into other divisions.   I
have counted them; there are *twenty-two* of them.
Each one contains *eight* verses, and each one has
a strange word over the top, such as *Aleph, Beth,
Gimel,* &c.   I have often wondered what this
meant.

Uncle. I can soon explain this.   But first let me
ask whether you know what an *acrostic* is ?

Hilary. O yes, we know that very well.   An
acrostic is a poem, in which the first letter of every
line being taken, makes up the name of some person.

Ernest. I have seen a poem of sixteen lines, in
praise of General Washington; and if you took all
the first letters of the lines together, they spelt
GEORGE WASHINGTON.

Uncle. Very well.   The 119th Psalm is a kind
of acrostic; not indeed in English, but in Hebrew.
If you can read Hebrew, I would show you that
every one of the eight verses begins with the same
letter.   And the name of that letter is placed at the
beginning of the division.

Hilary. Then these hard words, *Aleph*, *Beth*, and so on, are the names of the Hebrew letters?

Uncle. Exactly so. The old Hebrew alphabet contained *twenty-two* letters. Their names are Aleph, Beth, Gimel, &c. These names you will find set down in regular order in this psalm. Each of the first eight verses begins with some word which begins with *Aleph ;* each of the second set with *Beth*, and so on to the end.

Ernest. This is surprising, indeed. Are there any other parts of Scripture written in the same way ?

Uncle. Yes, this was a favourite method with the Hebrew poets.

Hilary. What was the use of this arrangement?

Uncle. I suppose it was meant to assist the memory. It is commonly used where there are a number of little unconnected sentences, or proverbs, which it would be difficult to recollect without some such aid. There are *twelve* of these acrostical poems in the Old Testament. In most cases, however, only a single verse begins with each letter.

Three of these passages are perfectly alphabetical, namely, Psalms cxi. and cxii. and the third chapter of Lamentations. Each line is marked by its initial letter. In the other nine passages, only every stanza is thus distinguished. These are

Psalms xxv. xxxiv. xxxvii. cxix. cxlv. Prov. xxxi. 10—31. Lam. i. ii. and iv.

Hilary. Then all these twelve poems must have been divided into verses from the first. Must they not?

Uncle. Yes, you are right. For the letters of the alphabet, with which every line or stanza began, separated it into a distinct verse. And now, as we have explained the difficulty about the 119th Psalm, we may proceed to something else.

Ernest. If you have nothing else to teach us just now, there is a question which I should like to ask.

Uncle. Ask it, my child.

Ernest. I have been turning over the leaves of this large English Bible on your table, and I see that it differs in some things from our small pocket Bibles.

Uncle. In what respects do you observe any difference?

Ernest. Why, sir, I see a line at the top of every column throughout the whole book. That is one difference. Please to look at the second page, over the second chapter of Genesis. Here are the words, *The first Sabbath.* And over the next column are the words, *The naming of the creatures.* And so on page after page—*The serpent tempteth Eve—Man is cast out of Paradise—The curses of Cain;* and so it continues through every book in the Bible.

Uncle. These little lines at the top of the page are called the " running-titles." They were made, I believe, by the same persons who translated the Bible. They are intended to show what is the subject of the verses below them. Thus, if you were looking through Exodus, to find when the Passover was instituted, you would have only to turn over the pages rapidly, reading the running titles ; and after turning over five or six leaves, you would come to the words *The Passover is instituted,* immediately over the 12th chapter. This would be just what you wished to find. In all complete copies of the Bible these running-titles are inserted, but they are omitted in many of the smaller and cheaper editions.

Ernest. I observe also at the beginning of every chapter in the whole Bible several lines of the same kind, in the same sort of type.

Uncle. I see what you mean. These are the *titles of the chapters.* They tell you what is contained in the chapter, and are a sort of *index* to the Scriptures. They answer the same purpose with the running-titles, but they are more full and comprehensive. Thus if you look at the 12th chapter of Exodus, to which you turned just now, and read the title, you will see what the chapter contains.

1. *The beginning of the year is changed.* 3. *The Passover is instituted.* 11. *The rite of the Passover.* 15. *Unleavened bread.* 29. *The first-born are slain.* 31. *The Israelites are driven out of the land.* 37. *They come to Succoth.* 43. *The ordinance of the Passover.*

Hilary. What do those little figures mean in the middle of the sentences?

Uncle. They show at what verse each subject begins; thus the figure 3 shows that the " institution of the Passover" is related at the *third* verse. So you perceive these titles of the chapters are very useful in helping us to find any particular passage. These also are left out in the smaller and cheaper editions.

Take notice that you may read these titles straight on, through a whole book, (omitting the numerals,) and you will thus have a little abridgement of all the book contains. Let us take, for example, the book of Ruth, because it is short. I will merely read the titles of the four chapters, without stopping.

" Elimelech, driven by famine into Moab, dieth there. Mahlon and Chilion, having married wives of Moab, die also. Naomi, returning homeward, dissuadeth her two daughters-in-law from going with her. Orpah leaveth her, but Ruth with great constancy accompanieth her. They two come to

Beth-lehem, where they are gladly received. Ruth gleaneth in the fields of Boaz. Boaz, taking knowledge of her, showeth her great favour. That which she got, she carrieth to Naomi. By Naomi's instruction, Ruth lieth at Boaz's feet. Boaz acknowledgeth the right of a kinsman. He sendeth her away with six measures of barley. Boaz calleth into judgment the next kinsman. He refuseth the redemption according to the manner of Israel. Boaz buyeth the inheritance. He marries Ruth. She beareth Obed, the grandfather of David. The genealogy of Pharez."

Here, you see, we have a little epitome of the whole history. And I have often found it useful, after I have finished the perusal of any book in the Bible, to go back, and read over all the titles of the chapters, in order to refresh my memory, and fix the connexion of events in my mind.

Hilary. Now, uncle, I have another thing which I wish to have explained. There is still something on every page of the large Bible which I do not find in our smaller ones. Down each side of every page there are a great many words in very small print. If you will look at the first chapter in the Bible, you will see what I mean. Just by the side of the first verse, on the left hand, I read

a John 1. 1, 2. Heb. 1. 10.
b Ps. 8. 3. & 33. 6. & 89. 11, 12.
& 102. 25. & 136. 5. &c.

And a little lower down, by the sixth verse, I read, Heb. *between the light and between the darkness.*

Uncle. All this, you perceive, is in the margin.

Hilary. What is meant by the *margin?*

Uncle. The *margin* is the *edge* of any thing. Thus the margin of a river is the edge of the river; the margin of a page is the edge of the page, which is commonly left blank. But sometimes there are little notes or explanations printed in this margin, either at the sides or at the bottom; and these are called *marginal notes.* The small print, which you observe at the sides of the page in the large Bible, is of three kinds. It consists, *first,* of *marginal readings,* or translations; *secondly,* of *marginal explanations;* and, *thirdly,* of *marginal references.*

Hilary. What do you mean by *marginal readings?*

Uncle. I will explain. In many cases, the Hebrew or the Greek text might be translated in two different ways. The translators were perhaps doubtful which was the best. They therefore placed one of these in the text, and the other in the margin. Sometimes also, the exact literal translation would sound very strange in English, and then they would put it into the margin.

Ernest. Please to explain this a little further.

Uncle. I will try to make myself understood. There are two sorts of marginal translations. And take notice they may be distinguished by the little word which precedes them. Every one of these little marginal readings begins, either with the letters *Heb.* or with the word *Or.* For example, look again at this first chapter of Genesis. There is a marginal reading at verse 4 ; it begins with the letters *Heb.* The marginal readings at verses 5, 6. 11. 14. 16. and 20, all begin with *Heb.* They are therefore of the first kind.

Hilary. What is there peculiar in this first kind of marginal readings?

Uncle. They are all exact, literal translations from the Hebrew or the Greek. As it is the same in both, I will confine myself to the Old Testament. Whenever you find a marginal note beginning with *Heb.*, you may know that it is a very literal translation from the Hebrew—often so literal that it would not sound right in English. The letters *Heb.* stand for *Hebrew,* and signify " In the original *Hebrew* it is" so and so. Thus look at the marginal note to the 4th verse ; it is as follows : Heb. *between the light and between the darkness.* This is a translation word for word from the Hebrew. But this does not sound well in English, and therefore the translation in the text is, " the light from the darkness."

In the New Testament, this first kind of marginal readings is just the same, except that *Gr.* is used instead of *Heb.* *Gr.* stands for *Greek*, in which language you remember the New Testament was written.

Hilary. Well, uncle, I think we understand about the first kind of marginal readings. They always begin with *Heb.* or *Gr.;* and they always contain a translation which is, word for word, like the Hebrew or Greek.

Uncle. Exactly right. Now you remember I told you of a second kind.

Ernest. Yes, sir; the second kind of marginal readings begins with the word *Or.*

Hilary. There is one in the chapter we have open. Gen. i. It is at verse 20.

Ernest. Here is another in the second chapter, at verse 14.

Uncle. Wherever the marginal reading is of this second kind, beginning with *Or*, the original admits of two different translations. One of them is put in the text; the other is put in the margin. Thus, in the first case, (Gen. i. 20,) the translation in the text is, the " moving" creature ; but the margin says " or creeping :" because the Hebrew word may be rendered either " moving" or " creeping." And in the second case, (Gen. ii. 14,) the translation in the text is, that is it which goeth " toward the east of" Assyria ; but the margin says " or *eastward to Assyria :*" because the Hebrew words may be rendered either way. And the sense is often very different.

Hilary. Is the translation in the margin by the same persons who made the other translation?

Uncle. The very same ; and is of equal authority. It is to be wished that every edition of the Scriptures had these marginal readings, because, in some instances, the best translation is placed in the margin.

Ernest. How did this happen? Did not the translators make the text as perfect as they could?

Uncle. There was, you know, a translation in common use before this was made. The people had a great affection for this old version, and did not like to see any alterations made. King James, therefore, commanded the translators to make no unnecessary changes in the old expressions. And, therefore, in many cases, they inserted the less correct version in the text, and placed the proper one in the margin, lest they should disturb the minds of common readers.*

---

* The first rule given by James I. to the translators was in these words : " The ordinary Bible read in the church, commonly called the Bishops' Bible, to be followed, and as little altered as the original will permit."

Hilary. It seems to me that these marginal readings are not in half our Bibles.

Uncle. That is, unhappily, true. Most of our American Bibles omit them. But they are of equal value with the other translation, and often afford great help in understanding a passage.

CHAPTER XII.

Marginal explanations continued—Dates — Abbreviations explained—Explanations of proper names—Brief comments Marginal references—Mode of using these—Use of parallel places exemplified—Recommended by Bishop Horsley—Good editions recommended—Use of Italics in the English Bible— Use of capitals—The word LORD—Use of brackets.

Hilary. THERE seem to be some other things in the margin which are not translations.

Uncle. Yes, you remember I told you before,* that besides the marginal readings, there were two other sorts of notes in the margin.

Ernest. I remember them ; marginal *explanations*, and marginal *references*.

Uncle. I have explained to you the marginal readings; now we will go on to the marginal *explanations*. Some of these give the *dates* of the transactions recorded. These are commonly at the top of the page, just under the running-title. I suppose you know what is meant by the *date* of a transaction.

Ernest. Yes, sir ; the time when any thing takes place.

---

* See page 144.

Uncle. Turn again to the first chapter of Genesis, and you will see over the top, " Before CHRIST, 4004." That is, the world was created four thousand and four years before the birth of our Saviour. Such dates you will find at every page.

Ernest. In the New Testament, the words are different. The words " Anno DOMINI" are at the top of each page.

Uncle. Anno Domini means, " In the year of our Lord," and then follows the number of years from Christ's birth. Thus in the Old Testament, we reckon *backwards* from the advent of Christ, and in the New Testament, we reckon *forwards* from the same point.

Hilary. In some places there is a syllable put before the number of the year. Over the eleventh chapter of Judges, it says, " Before CHRIST cir. 1143." What is meant by *cir.* ?

Uncle. I am always pleased to see you on the watch for something. *Cir.* stands for the Latin word *circiter*, which means *about.* That is, " *About* 1143 years before Christ;" for in many cases, the translators could not fix the exact date, but came as near to it as they could. And I will take this occasion to say, that learned men differ very much about the precise time when many other events took place. In a number of instances, the dates given at the top of the margin are thought to be incorrect : yet they are generally very useful, and we should have a much better understanding of what we read, if we more commonly took notice of them.

Ernest. Are these numbers always at the *top* of the column ?

Uncle. No. Often they are in the middle, or, indeed, in any other part of the margin. Thus in the eleventh chapter, there is a date given after every five or six verses.

But this is not the only kind of explanations which occur in the margin. There are also little remarks in various places, intended to explain some difficulty in the text. I will give you several examples. Look at Gen. v. 29, and you will find a note which tells you that the name *Noah* means *rest* or *comfort.* At Josh. xxiii. 34, we read that a certain altar was called *Ed ;* in the margin we read the meaning of the word, " That is, *witness.*" In Judg. vi. 24, another altar is called *Jehovah-shalom :* in the margin we read, " That is, the LORD *send peace.*"

Ernest. Are all these little remarks explanations of proper names ?

Uncle. Not all of them, though the greater number are ; for many of them are little comments on the text. Look at Judg. iii. 30, and you will find the remark : " It seems to concern only the country next the Philistines." And in the history of Jephthah, (Judg. xi. 29,) we read in the note. " Jephthah seems to have been judge only of North East Israel." So also you will find a longer note at 2 Kings xv. 1. And another at Hos. ix. 3 And again at Luke xix. 13, where an account is given of a nobleman who gave his servants " ten *pounds ;*" the marginal explanation says : " *Mina,* here translated a pound, is twelve ounces and a half : which, according to five shillings the ounce, is three pounds two shillings and sixpence."

Now we have gone over two kinds of marginal notes, first, *marginal readings or translations*, and secondly, *marginal explanations.* And these ex planations we found were of three sorts,—*dates, translations of proper names, and short observations.* A third kind of marginal notes still remains.

Ernest. Yes, uncle, *marginal references;* and I think I see them now, without having you to point them out to me. In the very first page, the small print by the first verse in the Bible ; are not these marginal references ?

Uncle. Yes. The words " a John 1. 1, 2. Heb. 1. 10," and all similar words are what I mean. These refer you to other texts in the Scrip- tures, which teach the same doctrine, or afford some useful explanation. Thus the first of these references is placed by the opening verse of Genesis : "In the beginning God created the heaven and the earth." And the reference in the margin is to John 1. 1, 2, which teaches the same truth: "In the beginning was the Word, and the Word was with God, and the Word was God. The same was in the beginning with God."

Hilary. What is the meaning of the little letter (a) prefixed to the reference?

Uncle. It points out what word or phrase in the text is particularly illustrated by the reference. Do you not see the same little letter in the text?

Hilary. O yes! I see a little *a* at the word " beginning."

Uncle. That is the portion of the text which is illustrated by John i. 1, 2. And if you look a little further you will see the letter *b*, before the phrase, " God created;" the same small letter in the margin refers you to the passages which teach the same doctrine.

Ernest. What is the use of these marginal references ?

Uncle. They point out other passages which help us to understand the text. Now, remember, these other passages are what are called *parallel passages ;* that is, passages which are alike—which teach the same thing—or which explain one another. And these are very useful ; for very often a thing is stated briefly in one passage, which is explained at length in another. Or a truth is partly expressed in one place, and fully expressed in an other. Or a statement is made in one passage, and some fact which makes it very clear is given in the parallel passage.

Ernest. Be so good as to give us an example.

Uncle. Turn then to the last verse of the first chapter of Hebrews.

Ernest. Heb. i. 14 : *Are they not all ministering spirits, sent forth to minister for them who shall be heirs of salvation ?*

Uncle. That teaches us that the angels are ministering spirits, or that they attend upon the children of God. Now look for the marginal references, in regular order.

Ernest. The letter *x* points out the first set. Gen. xix. 16. Yes, I see this text relates how two angels delivered Lot out of Sodom.

Hilary. Gen. xxxii. 1, 2. 24. These texts tell about the angels who met Jacob, and about the angel who wrestled with him.

Ernest. Ps. xxxiv. 7 : " The angel of the Lord encampeth round about them that fear him, and delivereth them."

Hilary. Ps. xci. 11 : " For He shall give his angels charge over thee, to keep thee in all thy ways."

Ernest. Ps. ciii. 20, 21 : " Bless the Lord, ye

his angels that excel in strength, that do his com-; mandments," &c.

Hilary. Dan. iii. 28. This speaks of an angel who delivered the three young men from the furnace.

Ernest. Dan. vii. 10 : " Thousand thousands ministered unto Him, and ten thousand times ten thousand stood before Him."

Uncle. You need not read any further. I am sure you see already the light which is thrown on Scripture, by examining the parallel texts.

Ernest. It seems to be almost as good as a commentary.

Uncle. Very often the parallel passages furnish the best commentary in the world.

This is so truly the case, that it is surprising how much knowledge of the Bible may be obtained by a common reader, who carefully makes use of all these marginal references. On this subject the learned Bishop Horsley says :

" It is incredible to any one who has not made the experiment, what a proficiency may be made in that knowledge which maketh wise unto salvation, by studying the Scriptures in this manner, *without any other commentary, or exposition, than what the different parts of the sacred volume mutually furnish for each other.* Let the most illiterate Christian study them in this manner, and let him never cease to pray for the illumination of that Spirit by which these books were dictated : and the whole compass of abstruse philosophy and recondite history shall furnish no argument with which the perverse will of man shall be able to shake this learned Christian's faith."*

Ernest. Now I believe we have finished all the three kinds of marginal notes. I will try to repeat them. *First, marginal readings;* which are either more exact translations from the Hebrew, or translations with another meaning. *Secondly, marginal explanations;* which are dates, or translations of proper names, or short observations. *Thirdly, marginal references,* or parallel passages.

Uncle. I wish you to observe that in our ordinary editions, these are all in the margin, but of late years a number of excellent editions of the Bible have appeared, with these marginal notes and references *between* the column. Such are Bagster's London Bibles, the Reference Bibles of the American Bible Society, and an edition published by the Society of Friends. All these are truly excellent editions.

Ernest. I have seen some Bibles which seem to have a much larger collection of references to parallel texts.

---

* Horsley's Nine Sermons, p. 224—238.

Uncle. True. The labour of biblical students has been constantly adding to the number, for many years. You would be surprised to learn how vast is the amount of these collections. To give you some idea of this, I will give you on a paper the names of certain editions of the Bible, with their respective dates, and the number of marginal references in each.

		Number of parallel texts.
First edition of	1611	9000
J. Haye's	1677	25,895
Dr. Scattergood's	1678	33,145
Bps. Tenison and Lloyd's.	1699	39,488
Dr. Blayney's.	1769	64,988
Bishop Wilson's.	1785	66,995

Besides these, I might mention Reference Bibles by the Rev. Dr. Thomas Scott, the Rev. Dr. Adam Clarke, and also those published by Mr. Bagster of London.

Ernest. There is another thing I wish to have explained. I have often taken notice that different sorts of print are used in the Bible. Why is this ?

Uncle. Ah ! you mean the Italics. But let me see whether you are acquainted with the difference between Roman and Italic letters. This sentence is in *Roman* type :

" He that hath no rule over his own spirit is like a city that is broken down, and without walls."

Ernest. Here is the same verse in *Italic* type :

" *He that hath no rule over his own spirit is like a city that is broken down, and without walls.*"

Hilary. Yes, I know the difference. The *Italic* letters lean a little more, and are shaped more like our common writing letters.

Uncle. Now look at the same verse in the twenty-fifth chapter of Proverbs, last verse:

" He that *hath* no rule over his own spirit *is like* a city *that is* broken down, *and* without walls."

Now tell me whether this is in Roman or Italic type.

Ernest. Partly in one, and partly in the other. The words *hath*—*is like*—*that is*—and *and,* are in Italics; all the rest are in Roman. Now what I want to learn is, why these words are in Italics?

Uncle. To show that they are not in the original, but are supplied by the translators in order to complete the sense. Very often, if a verse should be translated word for word, it would be scarcely intelligible in English. Read this passage, omitting the words in Italics, and you will perceive what I mean.

Hilary. " He that······no rule over his own spirit····a city····broken down····without walls."

Uncle. Wherever the translators insert a word which is not in the Greek or the Hebrew, they had it printed in this way. And this shows the remarkable honesty of our translation, where not even an "if" or an "and" is added, without being thus acknowledged. Commonly a few words only are added; but in some verses more are necessary. It is very important for every Bible reader to understand this use of Italics. For in other books, Italics are often employed to show that a particular emphasis is to be laid on the word thus printed. But in the Bible, the words in Italics are *never* emphatical.

Hilary. Are not the *marginal readings* also in Italics?

Uncle. Commonly they are so. But sometimes the marginal readings have words which are not in the original, and these are printed in Roman letters. Thus in 2 Chron. xx. 24, in the margin we read, "there was *not an escaping.*" The words "there was" are not in the Hebrew.

Ernest. I see how it is. The printing in the margin is exactly the reverse of the printing in the text.

Uncle. Precisely. What would be Roman in the text, is Italic in the margin; and what would be Italic in the text, is Roman in the margin.

Ernest. In many texts I see that some of the words are in large letters.

Uncle. Sometimes very important words are printed in *capitals.* The most remarkable case of this is the name LORD. You will observe that it is sometimes in small letters, and sometimes in capitals. It is in capitals only when the Hebrew word JEHOVAH is used in the original. This is the most awful name of God. It is supposed to signify the divine self-existence, eternity, and independence.

Ernest. This is something entirely new to me.

Uncle. And it is worthy of being remembered. Wherever you find the divine name LORD in small capitals, you may be sure that in the Hebrew it is JEHOVAH. But whenever it is in ordinary letters, there is some other name in the Hebrew.* You will see both names in the first verse of the eighth psalm : " O LORD our Lord, how excellent is thy name in all the earth !" Which might be read thus : " O Jehovah, our Lord, how excellent is thy name in all the earth !" Indeed, some learned men are of the opinion that the word *Jehovah* should have been retained in all places, as it has been in many.

Ernest. But capitals are used in printing some other words ; are they not ?

Uncle. They are ; as, for instance, when some divine name is mentioned, to which great attention ought to be paid. In Ex. iii. 14, we have one of the names of God : I AM THAT I AM. In Zech. vi. 12, Christ is called the BRANCH. In Jer. xxiii. 6,

---

* Commonly *Adonai.*

it is said, " And this is his name whereby he shall be called, THE LORD OUR RIGHTEOUSNESS."

Again, when an *inscription* or the quotation of some *title* is repeated, it is sometimes put in small capitals. You will better understand this from the examples. In Ex. xxxix. 30, we have the title or inscription which was engraved on the crown of the high-priest: HOLINESS TO THE LORD. In Zech. xiv. 20, we have the same inscription. In Dan. v. 25, we have the inscription on Belshazzar's wall: MENE, MENE, TEKEL, UPHARSIN. In Matt. xxvii. 37, we have the title which was placed over the head of our crucified Redeemer: THIS IS JESUS THE KING OF THE JEWS. This title was in three languages, and you will see other forms of it, in Mark xv. 26, Luke xxiii. 38, and John xix. 19. In Rev. xix. 16, we have the inscription which was on the vesture and the thigh of Messiah : KING OF KINGS AND LORD OF LORDS. All these are in capitals, and these may serve as examples. Indeed these are almost all the instances in the whole Bible.

Hilary. Now, uncle, I hope we are done with all that relates to the printing and type.

Uncle. There is only one little matter of this sort which remains. Look at the first epistle of John, second chapter and twenty-third verse.

Hilary. " Whosoever denieth the Son, the same

hath not the Father: [*but he that acknowledgeth the Son hath the Father also.*]

Ernest. Here is something more than Italics; here are ten words in a sort of parenthesis.

Uncle. Those ten words are enclosed in marks [ ] which are called *brackets.* These brackets show that the translators doubted whether the words between these marks belonged to the Scriptures.

Ernest. Why were they in any doubt about it?

Uncle. I suppose because it was wanting in the chief ancient manuscripts which they consulted. It is entirely wanting in the earlier English versions. But all learned commentators at this day agree that it does really form a part of holy Scripture, and therefore the brackets might be omitted.

And now, Hilary, we have finished all that relates to the type and printing. Though it may have been a little dry, it will prove useful to you through life. You may now go out, and divert yourselves with your Christmas plays.

CHAPTER XIII.

The dedication to King James—Tables at the end of the English
Bible—Proper names which are written differently in different places—Hard words in the book of Psalms—Selah, Hig-
gaion, etc.—Untranslated words—Hosanna, Tirshatha, etc.—
Obsolete words—List of these.

IT has always been observed, that the more diligently any one studies the Scriptures, the more
pleasure he takes in the study. Those who know
most about the Bible love it best. It is like a precious mine, in which the deeper we go the more
profitable do we find our labour. Our two little
boys already experienced the truth of this. They
had spent a good part of their Christmas holidays
in listening to their uncle's conversations about the
Bible, and yet they frequently said to one another
that they had never passed a vacation so agreeably.
As they were sitting by the fire in the study, the
next morning, before their uncle came in, Hilary
said to his brother, " Do you remember, Ernest,
that before we left New York I told you that I
wondered how our uncle could avoid being weary
of reading so much in the Bible ?"

Ernest. Yes, I remember it very well; but
what do you think about it now ?

Hilary. I do not wonder any longer, for I see that it is the most interesting book in all the world Every time I open my pocket Bible, I find something which I did not understand formerly, but which my uncle has explained to me.

Ernest. So do I. Now I know what is meant by the capitals, and the Italics, and the marginal readings, and this makes me take vastly more pleasure in the book than I ever could do before. But there are still two or three things which I wish to have explained.

Hilary. What are they?

Ernest. I will let you know as soon as our uncle comes in. O here he is already! Let us get our books and papers ready.

Uncle. Boys, are you ready for another lesson?

Hilary. Yes, sir, indeed we are, and Ernest has found out several other things in the English Bible which he does not understand.

Ernest. There is a *dedication* at the beginning of the Bible, and there are several *tables* at the close of the Old Testament. You have never said any thing about these.

Uncle. This is easily explained. You remember that I gave you a history of our English version, and told you that it was made by the order of King James the First. When the translators, therefore, had completed their work, they thought it right to dedicate it to their sovereign, and caused this dedication to be composed, and printed in the beginning of the Bible. It is placed in all English Bibles, and in such American Bibles as were printed before the Revolution. But it is now very properly omitted, as it contains nothing worthy of accompanying the word of God.

The *tables* of which you spoke are also by the translators, and they have been of great use to thousands of pious readers. There is a *Table of Scripture Measures*, which shows the value of the ancient measures used in the Bible, and giving us the amount in feet and inches, or in gallons and pints, or in bushels and pecks, as the case may be. Thus a *homer* is equal to seventy-five gallons, five pints, and a fraction. There is a *Table of Weights and Money*, and also a *Table of Time*. If you only know the rule in arithmetic called reduction, you may easily find, from this money table, how many dollars and cents are contained in any sum of money mentioned in Scripture.

The first editions of our English Bible contained a long and excellent preface by the translators, which has been omitted in later copies.

Ernest. I think I have observed that some proper names are different in the Old and New Testaments.

Uncle. That is true. And not only so, some

names are differently written in different places in the same Testament. For example, let Hilary read the eighth verse of the fourth chapter of Hebrews.

Hilary. " For if *Jesus* had given them rest, then would he not afterward have spoken of another day."

Uncle. Whom does the apostle mean by *Jesus?*

Ernest. I suppose he means the Lord Jesus.

Uncle. Not at all. He means *Joshua.* This person is called by four names in Scripture : Joshua, Jehoshua, Oshea, and Jesus. Acts vii. 45. Num. xiii. 8. 16. In order to assist you in your reading of the Scriptures, I will give you a little table of the principal names which appear in more than one form, with some references to the places. This paper you may copy, and lay it in your Bibles.

Achan, also called Achar. Josh. vii. 18. 1 Chron ii. 7.

Ai, Hai. Gen. xiii. 3. Josh. vii. 2.

Amos, Amoz. 2 Kings xix. 2. Isa. i. 1.

Asshur, Assur. Gen. x. 1. Hos. xiv. 3.

Askelon, Ashkelon. Judg. i. 8. Zech. ix. 5.

Azariah, Ozia, Uzziah. Matt. i. 8, 9. 2 Chron. xxvi. 1. 2 Kings xiv. 21.

Elijah, Elias. 1 Kings xvii. 1. Matt. xi. 14.

Elisha, Eliseus. Luke iv. 27. 1 Kings xix. 16.

Hadadezer, Hadarezer. 2 Sam. viii. 3. 1 Chron xviii. 3.

Hagar, Agar. Gen. xxi. 9. Gal. iv. 24.

Hezekiah, Ezekias. 2 Kings xvi. 20. Matt. i. 9.

Isaiah, Esaias. John xii. 39.

Jeremiah, Jeremy, Matt. xvi. 14. ii. 17.

Jehoahaz, Ahaziah. 2 Kings x. 35. 2 Chron. xx. 35.

Jonah, Jonas. Jonah i. 3. Matt. xii. 39.

Joram, Jehoram, Hadoram. 1 Chron. xviii. 10. 2 Kings viii. 16. 2 Sam. viii. 10.

Joshua, Jehoshua, Oshea, Jesus. Heb. iv. 8. Num. xiii. 8. 16.

Judah, Judas, Jude. Num. xxvi. 22. Matt. i. 2 Luke vi. 16. Jude i. 1.

Naashon, Naasson. Ex. vi. 23. Luke iii. 32.

Nebuchadnezzar, Nebuchadrezzar. Ezek. xxvi. 7. Jer. xxvii. 8.

Noah, Noe. Gen. vii 1 Luke xvii. 26.

Rabbah, Rabbath. Amos i. 14. Deut. iii. 11.

Saul, Shaul. Gen. xxxvi. 37. 1 Chron. i. 48.

Sidon, Zidon. Gen. x. 15. 1 Chron. i. 13.

Siloah, Siloam. Neh. iii. 15. John ix. 7.

Uriah, Urijah. Neh. iii. 21. 2 Sam. xi. 3.

Zachariah, Zechariah, Zacharias. Mal. xxiii. 35. Ezra v. 1. Luke i. 5.

Zion, Sion. 2 Sam. v. 7. Heb. xii. 22.

Ernest. Why is there this difference?

Uncle. Some of the differences are in the Hebrew, and cannot be accounted for now. Others arise from following the Hebrew spelling in the Old Testament, and the Greek in the New. Thus *Noe* is the Greek way of writing *Noah.* King James, in the third rule given to the translators, directed "the names of the prophets and the holy writers, with the other names in the text, to be retained as near as may be, accordingly as they are vulgarly used."

Ernest. Since our last conversation, I have observed several words in the book of Psalms, which I have never been able to understand.

Uncle. Repeat some of them.

Ernest. I mean such words as *Michtam, Aijeleth-Shahar, Shoshan-eduth, Selah,* &c.

Uncle. I perceive your difficulty. Most of these words occur in the *titles* of the Psalms, and they were left untranslated, because their signification could not be ascertained. If you read in a Reference Bible such as I have been describing, you will find in the margin the probable translation of many of these words. They are Hebrew words. Some of them are thought to refer to the contents of the psalm. Others are supposed to point out tunes or musical instruments. No word has ever perplexed learned critics more than SELAH, which is found seventy times in the Psalms, and three times in Habakkuk. Some of the wisest Jews have supposed it to be both a musical note, and a sign that there is something in the sense particularly deserving of the reader's meditation. But I should have to make a commentary if I were to dwell on the explanation of these difficulties, and must, therefore, advise you to look into the best notes on the Scriptures which you may have at hand.

You will also find in various parts of the English Bible, words which have either been left just as they are in the original, or only changed so far as to give them an English sound. Thus HOSANNA, which means, *Save, we pray thee;* ALLELUIA, or HALLELUJAH, which means *Praise the Lord;* TIRSHATHA, which means *governor;* AMEN, which means *verily,* or *be it so;* SABAOTH, which means *armies;* RACA, which means *worthless fellow;* BELIAL, which means *abandoned wickedness:* PROSELYTE, which means a *convert from the Gentiles;* PHYLACTERIES, which is the Greek for a superstitious inscription; BAPTISM, and BAPTIZE, of which the precise signification is a matter of difference among good Christians. However strange it may seem to find so many foreign words left untranslated by these learned men, you ought to be informed that the preceding versions, and also the

English versions now used by Roman Catholics, have a great many more.

Hilary. Will you be so obliging as to mention some of them ?

Uncle. Here are some of them : *Parasceve*, for preparation ; *Holocaust*, for whole burnt-offering ; *Pasche*, for passover; *Azymes*, for unleavened bread ; *Paraclete*, for Comforter ; *Neophyte*, for a new convert ; and many more.

Hilary. After all, uncle, I have some things still to inquire about. There are several places in the Bible where the expressions seem to me to be very odd ; so much so that I have often been ready to smile.

Uncle. Perhaps I foresee what you mean ; and if I do not mistake, you will find almost all these odd expressions to be phrases which were good English two hundred years ago, but which have now become obsolete.

Hilary. Pray, uncle, what do you mean by *obsolete ?*

Uncle. That which is worn out of use is *obsolete.* Any word which has ceased to be commonly used is said to be an *obsolete word.* Our language is perpetually changing ; old words are going into disuse, and new words are coming in by hundreds. So that no one need wonder that a book two centuries old should contain many expressions which are now obsolete. Some of these words are no longer used at all; others of them are no longer used in the same sense.

Hilary. I should like to have a specimen of such words; for I believe you have really hit upon just what I was about to say.

Uncle. It is easy to gratify you, as I have a list already made out. Although it is not complete, I hope it will answer your purpose.

OBSOLETE EXPRESSIONS IN THE ENGLISH BIBLE.

ADVISEMENT.—*Counsel, information.* 1 Chron. xii. 19.—Still used in law.

ALL TO.—*Quite.* Judg. ix. 53.—In the genuine English copies, it is printed *all too.* In Chaucer and Milton it is *al-to.*

ARTILLERY.—*Weapons.* Bows and arrows. 1 Sam. xx. 40.

BEWRAY.—*Betray, make known.* Prov. xxvii 16; xxix. 24. Isa. xvi. 3. Matt. xxvi. 73.—It is used by Spencer and Addison.

BRUIT.—*Report, noise.* Jer. x. 22. Nah. iii. 19.

CARRIAGE.—*Luggage, baggage.* Acts xxi. 15, " We took up our *carriages,* and went up to Jerusalem." Judg. xvii. 21. 1 Sam. xvii. 22, " David left his *carriage* in the hand of the keeper of the *carriage.*"

CHAPT.—*Cleft, opened.* Jer. xiv. 4.

CONEY.—*Rabbit.* Lev. xi. 5. Deut. xiv. 4. Ps. civ. 18. Prov. xxx. 26.

CORN.—*Grain.*—In America we employ the word *corn* exclusively to signify maize, or Indian corn. But in England it denotes any grain of which bread is made, such as wheat, rye, barley, &c.

COTE.—*Cot, cabin, enclosure.* 1 Sam. xxiv. 3 2 Sam. vii. 8. 1 Chron. xvii. 7. 2 Chron. xxxii. 28

DAYSMAN.—*Umpire, judge, referee.* Job ix. 33

EAR.—*Plough,* or *Till.*—This word comes from the Saxon *earrion,* to plough. Gen. xlvi. 6 " Neither *earing,* nor härvest." Ex. xxxiv. 21 Deut. xxi. 4. 2 Sam. viii. 21. Isa. xxxi. 24. It is found in Shakspeare. The old word *earable* was used for *arable.*

GOODMAN.—*Master.* Matt. xx. 11.

HALE.—*Haul, drag.* Luke xii. 58. Acts viii. 3. —Used by Shakspeare and Milton.

HIS.—*Its.*—The possessive pronoun " its" is not used in the English version. Gen. i. 25, &c.

KERCHIEF.—*Head-dress.* Ezek. xiii. 18—21.

LEASING.—*Lying.* Ps. iv. 2 ; v. 6.

NEESINGS.—*Sneezings.* Job xli. 18.

OR EVER.—*Before.* Dan. vi. 24.

POLL.—*The head.* Num. i. 2. 18. 20. 22 ; iii. 47. 1 Chron. xxiii 3. 24.—*To poll* signifies to cut the hair off the *poll* or head. 2 Sam. xiv. 26 Ezek. xliv. 20. Mic. i. 16.

PREVENT.—To *go before;* to *anticipate.*—This word is now always used in the sense of *to hinder*, but in almost every instance in the English Bible it signifies to " be beforehand" with some person or thing. Ps. lix. 10 ; cxix. 148. Matt. xvii. 25. 1 Thess. iv. 15.

SEETHE.—*Boil.* 2 Kings iv. 38.

SERVITOR.—*Servant.* 2 Kings iv. 39.

SHROUD.—*Shelter.* Ezek. xxxi. 3.

SILVERLINGS.—*Pieces of silver money.* Isa.vii.23.

SITH.—*Since.* Ezek.. xxxv. 6.

STEAD.—*Place.* 1 Chron. v. 22.

STRAIT.—*Narrow, close.*—This word must be carefully distinguished from *straight.* 2 Kings vi. 1. Isa. xlix. 20. Matt. vii. 13. Luke xiii. 24:

TACHE.—*Loop, hole, latch.* Ex. xxvi. 6. 11.33 ; xxxv. 11 ; xxxvi. 13 ; xxxix. 33.

THRUM.—*The ends of weavers' threads.*—Used in the margin. Isa. xxxviii. 12. It is found in Shakspeare.

TIRE.—*Attire, dress:* 2 Kings ix. 30. Ezek. xxiv. 17.

WHILES.—*While.*

WHIT.—*A particle, an atom.* 1 Sam. iii. 18. John vii. 33 ; xiii. 10. 2 Cor. xi. 5.

WIMPLE.—*Veil.* Isa: iii. 22.

WIT, or WOT.—*Know.* 2 Cor. viii. 1. " We do you to *wit*," signifies " We inform you."

CHAPTER XIV.

Certain preliminary knowledge which is necessary in order to understand the Scriptures—Supposed case of a Chinese Life of Washington—Ancient geography—Chronology—Manners and customs of the East.

On a pleasant winter's evening, after the boys had been spending most of the day in a sleigh-ride to a neighbouring village, they were called into their uncle's study. The windows were closed, and a bright fire was burning on the hearth. The sofa was wheeled round, and two cheerful lamps were placed upon a table, which was covered with books, maps, and pictures. Uncle Austin signified that he wished them to take their seats on each side of him, and Ernest and Hilary awaited, with faces of happy expectation, the instructions which seemed to be prepared for them. Their good teacher began as follows :

Uncle. My lads, are you fond of history ?

Hilary. O yes, sir, we have read several histories.

Uncle. What histories have you read ?

Ernest. I can hardly tell you, without considering, they are so many. There is Goldsmith's History of Greece, and of Rome, and of England ; and

Scott's Tales of a Grandfather; and the History of the Jews.

Hilary. Yes, and Irving's Life of Columbus, and the Life of General Washington.

Uncle. All very good. Now let me ask you a question or two. Which of these do you like the most?

Ernest. I think I like the last one best.

Hilary. I am *sure* I do. Washington was the father of his country. I love to read about him—I love to see his very name. We have read his life three or four times over.

Uncle. Very well. Now suppose this history should last for three thousand years from this time. Suppose the English language in which it is written should cease to be spoken. And suppose that certain people on the other side of the globe, for example in China, should by some means get a copy of this same Life of Washington; do you think they would receive as much pleasure from it as you now receive?

Ernest. O no! certainly not.

Uncle. And why not?

Ernest. Because they would not be able to un derstand English.

Uncle. But suppose some very learned man should translate it into Chinese; do you think the

youth of China would take as much pleasure in it
as you do in the original?

Hilary. I do not know. It is a thing I never
thought of before.

Ernest. No, sir; they would find it hard to
know what it meant; and I imagine they could not
feel much interest in it.

Uncle. What difficulty would they have in understanding it, supposing it were in their own language?

Ernest. Why, perhaps they would not know
any thing about America, and the history is almost
all about things in America. When they read about
the battles of Yorktown, and Princeton, and Tren-
ton, they would not know where these places were,
or how far they were from one another.

Uncle. Exactly so; and the only way to comprehend these things would be, to give them some
idea of American geography. Now do you not
suppose that there are many readers of the English
Bible, who know quite as little about the geography of Palestine and other eastern countries?

Ernest. No doubt there are many such. I am
afraid I am one of the sort myself; for in reading
the Bible, I find myself often at a loss to know
where the events which are related took place.

Uncle. Now you have come exactly to the place
whither I was leading you. I like to make you

teach yourself. Impress this point on your mind, that *Sacred Geography* is of the utmost importance, in order to render the Scriptures either plain or profitable. This is the *first* thing we have learned this evening.

Many persons read the Bible, year after year, without ever taking the trouble to inquire whereabout the places mentioned in it are situated. Yet there are numerous passages which have little meaning to one who does not attend to the geography ; and other passages which have peculiar beauty when we have the whole position of the scene in our minds.

Ernest. Please to mention one or two of these.

Uncle. I will give you an example of the advantages of biblical geography. You have often read the account of the journeyings of the Israelites.

Ernest. O yes! They travelled from Egypt into Canaan.

Hilary. Yes, and they were forty years making this journey.

Uncle. Now did you ever take notice of the direction in which they travelled ?

Ernest. Let me consider. Egypt lies southwest of Canaan. Indeed, I never thought much about it, but I suppose they must have travelled towards the northeast.

Uncle. And how far was it from the northeast

part of Egypt to the part of Canaan which they
first entered ?

Ernest. I never thought of the distance.

Uncle. I will show you. Look at this little
map. Here is a view of the track of the Israelites.
Instead of going directly towards the northeast, you
see they made a great circuit.

First they went southeast to the Red Sea. Then
they pursued their way still more towards the south,
along one branch of the Red Sea. Then they turned
towards the north by Mount Sinai, through the
Desert of Paran. Then to the northeast, until they
approached the southern part of Palestine. Here
they might have entered ; but the Lord caused them
to turn directly back, and journey southward again,
by Mount Hor, to the point of the eastern branch
of the Red Sea. Then they turned northward once
more, and pursued that general direction until they
came to their journey's end.

Ernest. And this is the reason why they were
so long in making the journey ?

Uncle. Yes. At some of these places they were
made to remain months, and perhaps years. Much
of the time they were wandering about in the wilder-
ness. So that they were forty years in accom-
plishing a journey which they might otherwise
have accomplished in forty days.

Ernest. I have often thought, in reading the

history of the apostle Paul, that I should be very glad to have a map in which I could see the course which he took in his voyages and travels.

Uncle. There are many such maps; and I have several in which there are lines showing how he went from place to place in his five principal journeys. One of these maps has each of these tracks marked with a distinct colour, which prevents all confusion.* I would advise you, whenever you study the Scriptures, to have at hand good maps of all the places named; and also a plan of the city of Jerusalem, such as you see over the fireplace. Examine these carefully; seek out all the principal places; and by degrees you will get these so fixed in your mind, that you will scarcely need your maps any more.

Ernest. I see very plainly that a knowledge of the places mentioned in Scripture is very necessary.

Uncle. Perhaps I may find time to speak more largely on this subject. At present, it is sufficient to repeat what I just said, that you ought to make it a point to learn where every place lies, concerning which you read in the Bible. This can be acquired with less labour and in less time than you

---

* Maps of this kind are published by the American Sunday-school Union.

now suppose. The knowledge of biblical geography will make many dark places clear. It will enable you to accompany the personages in sacred history in all their travels ; and, besides adding to your delight in the word of God, will fix what you read in your memory.

But let me return to the supposition about the Chinese version of Washington's Life. Suppose some young mandarin in the city of Nankin should be busily engaged in the perusal of this volume, and suppose likewise, that by the help of some missionary he had been able to acquire a little notion of American geography, would every thing then become plain ?

Hilary. I imagine many things might be a great deal plainer than they could have been before, but still he might not be able to tell exactly *when* all these events happened. Uncle, am I not right ?

Uncle. You are, my dear boy. And this knowledge of *when* such and such things happened, is precisely the thing I wish you to consider. This knowledge of *the time when* events took place is what is called *Chronology*. Chronology teaches the times when all great historical facts occurred. Sacred chronology, or biblical chronology, teaches the times when those events which the Bible relates occurred.

Ernest. So we have another important thing to learn, besides geography.

Uncle. Yes. Fix it well in your mind; that biblical chronology is of great importance in order to render the Scriptures either plain or profitable. This is the *second* thing we have learned this evening.

When I was a boy, I read much in the Bible, and finding the book of Matthew placed immediately after the book of Malachi, that is, finding the New Testament beginning just where the Old Testament ends, I never dreamed that there was a period of more than four hundred years between the writing of these two books.

Hilary. Four hundred years! Can it be possible?

Uncle. It is truly so. And during this period, some most important events took place. But I cannot dwell on these at present. I will take another example. How many years is it since Jesus Christ was born?

Hilary. Eighteen hundred and thirty-eight.

Uncle. Very well: so it is, according to the common reckoning. Now, would it not help you to understand the gospel, if you knew exactly how long this was after the creation—how many years before Jerusalem was destroyed—how many years after the great city of Rome was built? Also, would it not be very pleasant to know what was happening in other parts of the world at this very time—what kings were reigning—what great generals were alive—who were the learned men—and the like ?

Ernest. O, I see at once how much good this would do, though I never thought of it before.

Uncle. Very well. Chronologers have made lists of all great events, putting down the times when they occurred. These lists are called chronological tables. Some of them are so large as to fill great volumes. Others are smaller, and record only the principal events ; and some are made still smaller, so as to give only what is necessary for the understanding of the Bible.

If you look at this large chronological map or table, you will perceive several interesting particulars about the time of our Lord's incarnation. For example, Christ was born seven hundred and fifty-three years after the building of Rome ; seventy years before the destruction of Jerusalem.

At this time, Augustus had been reigning more than twenty-six years as Roman emperor. Virgil had been dead fourteen years, Horace three years, Livy and Ovid were still alive. The Romans were at peace with all nations, and continued so for about three years. All this is interesting, and I might tell you many more things which were remarkable at that very time. All this is to be found in books of chronology.

Hilary. But must we read through all these great, dry volumes?

Uncle. I hope, before long we shall have some pleasant tables of chronology, prepared for the use of Bible scholars. But our common Bibles give us much assistance on these very points. I have frequently told you how desirable it is to read the Scriptures in an edition that has every thing in it which the excellent translators furnished, namely, the marginal notes and readings, the references, and the dates. These *dates* answer the purpose of a chronological table. Open the Bible which lies on the stand, and tell me what edition it is.

Ernest. It is a stereotype edition, printed at New York, for the American Bible Society, in the year 1834.

Uncle. Look at the bottom of the title-page on the left hand, and you will find a few small letters.

Ernest. I see them; they are these, 12*mo. ref.*

Uncle. That means *duodecimo Reference Bible.* It is an excellent Bible for those whose eyes are good. For elderly people there is a larger one, of the size called *octavo ;* and another still larger, of the size called *quarto.* All these are exactly alike except in size and shape. Now look at the top of the middle column, and you will observe the *dates.*

Ernest. Yes, I see them. Now I understand

you, and I will take care to observe these whenever I read.

Uncle. But now I have still another question to propose. If the young Chinese scholar were well informed as to the part of the world where Washington lived, and the exact time of his birth and death; do you think this would remove all difficulties in reading the history? In other words, would he be likely to understand the book as well as one relating to his own country?

Ernest. I think not. There would still be one difficulty. I scarcely know how to express myself; but every thing in this country is so different from what it would be China, that I think he would be at some loss to know what the book meant.

Uncle. Explain yourself more fully.

Ernest. I mean this; our dress is different from that of China. The young Chinese would not understand the names of our garments. Our houses and roads are different; our religion is different; and our government is different; so that I do not see how he could perfectly understand the book without information on these subjects.

Uncle. You have discovered exactly what I meant. In order to understand any work, it is necessary that we should be acquainted with the manners and customs of the people to whom it relates. Now observe, the books which compose the Bible were written some centuries ago; and they relate to a people whose manner of life was exceedingly unlike our own. The inhabitants of the East differ greatly in their manners from the people of Europe and America; and every book in the Bible abounds in allusions to these peculiarities. In order to arrive at what the Scriptures mean, we must therefore make ourselves acquainted with the particulars in which the life and habits of the Orientals vary from our own. This is called Oriental Antiquities; or, with reference to the Bible, *Biblical Antiquities*. In our next conversation, I will give you a number of interesting facts on this subject.

Before we separate for the evening, let me see whether you remember what I have been teaching you. I have mentioned to you three things, the knowledge of which is necessary in order to the intelligent study of the Scriptures. What are these three things?

Hilary. First, *Biblical Geography*.

Secondly, *Biblical Chronology*.

Thirdly, *Biblical Antiquities*.

Uncle. Very well answered. And now we shall prepare for our evening worship, for I suppose you begin to think of going to rest.

CHAPTER XV.

Illustrations from Biblical Antiquities—Difference between eastern and western manners—Oriental houses—Posture at meals—Manner of sitting—Eastern dress—Girdles—Eastern bottles—Tear-bottles—Funerals—Phylacteries.

THE little boys remembered the promise of their uncle, that in the next conversation he would proceed to give them some interesting particulars about the customs of the East. They hastened into his study the next morning at an earlier hour than usual, to remind him of his engagement, and were received by him with a smiling countenance. His large table was covered with heavy books, pictures, and a number of curiosities which looked as if they had come out of a museum. Ernest and Hilary seated themselves near the cheerful fire, and the good old gentleman began thus :

Uncle. I am now about to tell you a number of things which will be very entertaining ; and which relate to the antiquities of the Hebrews. I have on this table several books written by learned men who have travelled in the Holy Land and other eastern countries. Here are likewise a number of large plates which will give you a good idea of many objects spoken of in Scripture ; and besides, several of the real things, which you shall presently have in your hands.

Hilary. O that will be delightful !

Uncle. Observe it is not my purpose merely to amuse you, but to impress on your minds this principle, that *a knowledge of the manners and customs of the East throws great light upon the Scriptures.*

Every nation has its own manners and customs, differing more or less from those of all other nations. Those people who live furthest apart are generally most unlike. The inhabitants of a very warm climate are very different from those of a cold climate. The habits and practices of the same people greatly vary during the course of one or two thousand years. We should, therefore, expect to find the people mentioned in the Bible differing in many important respects from ourselves. I am about to mention a few of these differences ; it would take me weeks to mention them all. Books of travels and works on antiquities will teach you all that is necessary for you to know. Bear this always in mind when you are reading the Scriptures, that you must, as far as possible, forget the peculiarities of our own time and nation, and try to feel as if you were Hebrews.

Hilary. I suppose they never had such cold weather as this in Judea.

Uncle. Not for any length of time. Although the nights are often cold, yet snow and ice are very rare. It may be called a hot climate. The part of the land which lies on the Mediterranean is often fanned with cooling breezes ; and there is a refreshing atmosphere upon the mountains ; but in the vale of Jordan, and other inland parts, it is often excessively hot. In our climate, we never can foretell when it will rain ; but in Palestine the rain falls periodically. They have what they call the *former* and the *latter* rain, and these last for many days together. They are sometimes so severe as to beat down the houses of the poor, which are often made of palm branches, mud, and tiles, dried in the sun.

Ernest. That puts me in mind of what our Saviour says : " And the rains descended, and the floods came, and the winds blew, and beat upon that house, and it fell, and great was the fall thereof."*

Uncle. Very true ; and thus you see how the knowledge of this fact explains the text. But there are a thousand such cases.

Hilary. Be so good as to mention a few of the things in which we differ from the Hebrews.

Uncle. That is what I propose to do. In the first place, our way of living is very unlike their's

* Matt. vii. 27.

We live altogether in solid houses, of brick, stone, or strong wood. The Hebrews, in many cases, dwelt in tents, as the Arabs do to this day.

Hilary. But had they no houses?

Uncle. O yes; but their houses differed very much from ours. There are very few wooden houses in these countries, because forest trees are scarce. There are scarcely any houses of three stories, and few of more than one. The outside of their houses is very plain, often unsightly, and on the side next the street there are few windows, and often none at all.

In America, all our dwellings have sloping roofs; but the Hebrews had flat roofs. They spent much of their time on these roofs, which were sometimes covered with clay. There were little walls or parapets to keep any one from falling off. In our houses, the only way of getting to the roof is through the inside of the building; but the Hebrew houses often had stairs on the outside leading to the housetop. And this way explains what our Lord means when he says, "Let him which is on the *housetop* not come down to take any thing out of his house."* The Hebrews used to sleep during a great part of the year on these flat roofs. The Arabs and Syrians do so still. Dr. Pococke,

---

* Matt. xxiv. 17.

(who wrote this large work,) tells us, that " when he was at Tiberias in Galilee, he was entertained by the sheik's (or governor's) steward, and that they supped on the top of the house for coolness, according to their custom, and lodged there like-wise, in a sort of closet, about eight feet square, of a wicker work, plastered round toward the bottom, but without any door, each person having his cell." This was in the month of May.

In our houses we have fire-places and chimneys; the Hebrews had nothing of the sort. Neither had they any thing like our glass windows. Another

peculiarity in the eastern houses is, that they generally have a considerable space in the middle of
them, which is open at the top. This is called the
inner court. In the centre of this, rich persons
sometimes had one or more fountains playing, as
seen in the engraving.

Ernest. All this would seem very strange to us ;
yet I remember several things in the Scriptures
which this explains.

Uncle. Moreover, when you enter an eastern
house, you find every thing very unlike what you
are accustomed to. We usually take three meals
a day, the Hebrews took but two. We sit upon
chairs around a table. The Orientals, properly
speaking, have neither chair nor table. They sit
on the floor, or on a mat, cushion, or very low
seat, and have the food placed near them in trays
or on boards. We use knives and forks. The Hebrews used neither, but thrust their hands into the
dish, and pulled the meat apart with their fingers.

Hilary. This does not seem to me to be very
cleanly.

Uncle. You must remember that the Orientals
keep their hands exceedingly clean. Besides their
other ablutions, they carefully wash their hands
before and after every meal.

Ernest. But do not the eastern people make
any use of chairs ?

Uncle. No. The rooms of those who are wealthy are furnished with costly carpets or mats, and on these they sit down cross-legged. But along the wall of the room, there is frequently a little stage or platform, raised a few inches, or perhaps a foot or two, and here they have their beds ; here they also sometimes sit or recline during the day. This is called the *divan.* The most honourable place is in the corner.

Ernest. But I think I have been told that the ancients used to lie down at their meals.

Uncle. In early times the Hebrews did not practise this method, but it certainly was in use at the time of our Saviour's ministry, and was probably borrowed from the Greeks and Romans. The early Greeks and Romans used to sit at their meals, but after they became more luxurious they introduced this way of reclining at table. In a beautiful picture under article *Feast,* in the UNION BIBLE DICTIONARY, you have the representation of a Roman company reclining at a feast. You will see many of them have their heads adorned with wreaths, which was customary when they drank wine. You will also see gladiators, or swordsmen, fighting for the amusement of the company ; a cruel entertainment practised among the Romans. The Jews in our Saviour's time, following this example, used to lie on long couches, like sofas, when they ate.

These couches were covered with soft cushions and pillows. They lay on the left side, and in eating used only the right hand. As they thus lay around the table, their feet would of course extend back from it, so that a person might go around the company, and touch the feet of every one at the table. In this way, the woman in the gospel came behind and washed our Lord's feet with her tears. When they reclined near to one another, one person often leaned on the bosom of the next. In this way the beloved disciple leaned upon the bosom of Christ. But you will comprehend this whole subject better by means of a picture which you will find under article *Eat* in the UNION BIBLE DICTIONARY. There you will plainly see how the feet of any guest might be approached; and also how any person, reclining near one of the corners, might be said to lie in the bosom of the next one.

Ernest. I have observed in reading the Bible that the dress of the eastern people is very different from ours.

Uncle. Yes, so much so that there are many passages of Scripture which it is scarcely possible to understand without a knowledge of the ancient oriental apparel. The dress of those countries is adapted to a warm climate; and it is observed that they do not change their fashions every few months, as we do, but wear very much the same sort of clothes from age to age.

We are accustomed to see people clothed in garments which are cut rather tight, so as to show the shape; but the Hebrews were more fond of flowing robes, for men as well as women. We wear hats, but the Orientals wear turbans, or other headdresses of cloth. We are careful to shave off our beards; the Hebrews cherished the beard as their greatest ornament and honour. We cover our feet with stockings, shoes, and boots; the Hebrews went barefoot, or used light sandals; in no case making use of stockings. The eastern women are not content with ear-rings, but wear precious rings in the nose also. They colour their eyelids and their nails, and have ornaments upon their wrists and ankles.

Ernest. We read a great deal about the *girdle;* what was it like?

Uncle. As the garments of the Hebrews hung about them in a loose and flowing manner, they needed some sort of band or belt to keep them in place. This was the girdle. In the house this was seldom necessary, but when they were at work, or on a journey, or going to battle, their long robes would have been a great hinderance, unless they were tucked up and secured by this band.

Whenever a man was in great haste or activity,

he fastened the girdle closely around his body ; this was called " girding up the loins." So when Elijah predicted the rain, he " *girded up his loins* and ran before Ahab."* And when our Saviour was about to wash the feet of his disciples, " he took a towel and girded himself."†

Hence girding the loins came to be used to mean preparation for active service. Thus Christ says to his disciples, " let your loins be *girt about*, and your lights burning ;"‡ that is, be in a state of constant preparation.

Hilary. There is a verse in the gospel of Matthew which I never could understand, and I wish you would explain it to me. It is said, " Neither do men put new wine into old bottles ; else the bottles break, and the wine runneth out, and the bottles perish : but they put new wine into new bottles, and both are preserved."§ I never could see why an old bottle should break because it had new wine in it.

Uncle. Here is a case that shows how necessary it is to have some knowledge of eastern customs. If the bottles meant were of glass or earth, such as we use, the text would be without meaning ; and some ignorant infidels have ridiculed it as being

---

* 1 Kings xviii. 46. † John xiii. 4.
‡ Luke xii. 36. § Matt. ix. 17.

absurd. But the Hebrews used a sort of bottle with which we have no acquaintance ; their bottles were of skins.

Hilary. Of skins ! I never heard of such a thing.

Uncle. It is nevertheless true ; and the eastern people use the same in our day. They prepare the skin of a kid or goat in such a way as to make it hold liquids, and find them very convenient. Let me read you a passage from the travels of Sir John Chardin.

" They put into these goat and kid skin vessels every thing which they want to carry to a distance in the East, whether dry or liquid, and very rarely make use of boxes and pots, unless it be to preserve such things as are liable to be broken. The reason is, their making use of beasts of carriage for conveying these things, who often fall down under their loading, or throw it down ; and also because it is in pretty thin woollen sacks that they enclose what they carry. There is another advantage, too, in putting the necessaries of life in these skin vessels ; they are preserved fresher."

I will now show you a little picture from the Antiquities of Herculaneum. Here you see a woman pouring wine into a cup from just such a bottle. You may perceive that after the skin has been taken from the animal, and suitably dressed, the places where the legs were have been stopped

up. This cut will give you a better idea of an ancient bottle than any description of mine.

This will enable you to understand another passage which occurs in the book of Joshua. You remember that when the Israelites were destroying the nations of Canaan, the people of Gibeon came to Joshua, and pretended that they lived at a much greater distance than the others. They came with old tattered clothes, "*and wine-bottles, old and rent, and bound up.*"* Now a person ignorant of what I have been telling you could not comprehend how a bottle could be *torn*, or *bound up;* but all this is very intelligible when you learn that these bottles were made, not of glass, but of skin.

Hilary. But still, uncle, I do not see why the

* Josh. ix. 4. 13.

putting of new wine into an old skin should break it.

Uncle. Let me explain this. When wine is new it ferments, and every fermenting liquor swells, and requires more room. This is what causes so many porter-bottles to burst. Now if this new wine be put into a fresh, new skin, which is soft and flexible, the skin will yield and stretch as the liquor swells with fermentation, and no injury will be done. But if the same lively liquor be put into bottles of old skins, which have become dry and stiffened, they will not be able to stretch and make room, but will crack and burst, and let the wine run out.

Ernest. O, how plain that makes it! I am determined to read a great deal more about Hebrew customs. I had no idea that it was so entertaining.

Uncle. Indeed there are few studies so truly amusing as well as instructive. Besides, you may be pursuing these inquiries all your life. I never meet with a new book of travels in the East which does not add something to my knowledge of the Bible.

I will now ask you a question or two: What does the psalmist mean when he says, *I am become as a bottle in the smoke?**

---

* Ps. cxix. 83.

Ernest. I suppose he means that he was with-
ered and wrinkled by care and distress, just as a
goat-skin bottle is drawn up and injured by being
smoked.

Uncle. Very well: here is another question.
David addresses God, in prayer, thus: *Put thou
my tears into thy bottle.** What does this mean?

Ernest. I confess I have no idea.

Hilary. Nor I.

Uncle. The allusion here is to a very singular
custom of the ancients. We are not well informed
of what the Hebrews did, but the Greeks and Romans, when they wept for the death of any dear
friend, used to catch the tears in little phials, and
offer them upon the tomb of the deceased. These
were called *lacrymatories*, or tear-vessels. In
opening tombs in Italy many of these lacrymatories
have been found. I remember to have seen several
in Peale's Museum at Philadelphia; and I have
examined pictures of a great many. They were
made sometimes of baked earth, sometimes of glass,
and sometimes of precious stones, such as agate or
sardonyx. The meaning, therefore, of the psalmist's prayer is, ' Remember my griefs, as the tears
of mourners are preserved.'

I will now show you cuts of two Roman lacrymatories, found near Naples.

---

* Ps. lvi. 8.

Hilary. They seem to have had very strange customs at their funerals.

Uncle. Yes, the ancient methods of showing grief were very different from ours, and far more violent. Every eastern funeral is attended by a great number of women, who fill the air with shrieks and wailings. Sometimes persons are hired for this purpose. Every passenger who goes along thinks it meritorious to join in these lamentations. Perhaps this may explain a text in Jeremiah : " Call for the *mourning women*, that they may come ;········ and let them make haste, and take up a wailing for us, that our eyes may run down with tears, and our eyelids gush out with waters."*

Ernest. There is something like this in the Gos-

---

* Jer. ix. 17, 19.

pels, where Christ went to bring to life the daughter of a certain ruler. When he came into the house, he " saw the minstrels and the people making a noise."* But what were the *minstrels?*

Uncle. The word translated *minstrels* signifies players on the flute or pipe. These were employed at funerals, to play mournful tunes. Josephus tells us of a great mourning at which "many *hired pipers* led the way in the wailings."†

Hilary. While you are talking about Hebrew customs, I beg you will explain to me one word which has always perplexed me very much. Our Saviour says of the Pharisees : " They make broad their *phylacteries.*"‡

I do not know the meaning of this word.

Uncle. This word occurs only in this one text. It means a *preservative*, or amulet, and the thing was used by the superstitious Jews to protect them from evil. The phylacteries were little boxes or rolls of parchment which they wore about their persons; sometimes on their foreheads, and sometimes on their wrists. These little articles had texts of the law written on them; especially four passages.§

---

* Matt. ix. 23.   † Josephus' Wars, book iii.
‡ Matt. xxiii.
§ Ex. xiii. 2—10; 11—16. Deut. vi. 1—9; xi. 13—21.

Hilary. Why did they wear these texts on their persons ?

Uncle. In this, as in innumerable instances, they unwisely took the commands of the law in their most literal signification. You may remember that the Lord had spoken thus to them : " And it shall be for a sign upon thy hand, and for a memorial between thine eyes :"* and again, " Thou shalt bind them for a sign upon thine hand, and they shall be as frontlets between thine eyes."† In consequence of misunderstanding these texts, the Pharisees actually fastened fragments of the law upon their bodies. They were written on little pieces of parchment, which were rolled up, or enclosed in small square boxes, both being tied on with strings. You will have a good idea of them by looking at the engraving under article *Phylacteries* in UNION BIBLE DICTIONARY. Those Pharisees who wished to make a great show of their religion used to wear these hypocritical ornaments very large ; and it was this which our Saviour intended to rebuke For the reverence which we ought to feel for the word of God, is not to be displayed by wearing parts of it on our face and hands ; but by loving it, studying it, and conforming ourselves to its holy contents.

---

* Ex. xiii. 9.   † Deut vi. 8.

I hope I have now said enough to show you the great importance of being acquainted with biblical antiquities. It is a delightful study, and a number of books have been published, which contain all the facts which it is necessary for you to know. These you may read as you grow older.

Ernest. My dear uncle, we have now been here more than three weeks, and in a few days we shall have to return to New York. I have been thinking how pleasant it would be, if you would give us a few directions for reading the Scriptures. These would be very useful to us, when we are at home.

Uncle. The same thought has occurred to my own mind, and I have actually prepared a paper containing a number of directions, which you and Hilary may copy, and take home with you. But more of this to-morrow.

CHAPTER XVI.

Rules for the reading of Scripture :—The Bible must be read as
the Word of God—With prayer for divine light—Diligently—
Patiently—Attentively—With faith—With obedience—With
self-application—With fervour—At hours of devotion—With
Christ always in view—More than other books.

AFTER having spent most of the day in active
exercise, the boys hastened into the study, and
found their uncle seated and waiting for them. He
took a paper from his desk, and putting on his
spectacles, began as follows.

Uncle. My children, I have here a paper containing a number of directions for the study of the
Scriptures. But in order that you may be at no
loss to understand what they mean, I will read
them over to you, one by one, and explain them.

Ernest. Suppose we take pen and ink, and
write them down as you proceed.

Uncle. Very well. That will be very proper, as
it will serve to fix them in your memories.

Now get your paper ready, and we will begin

Direction I.

IN ALL YOUR READING OF THE BIBLE, BEAR
IN MIND THAT IT IS THE WORD OF GOD.

You must never forget that this book is the only

book in the world which has come directly from God. Holy men of old wrote these things by the inspiration of the Holy Ghost. Do you not remember a text which teaches this?

Hilary. Yes, sir. " All Scripture is given by inspiration of God, and is profitable for doctrine, for reproof, for correction, for instruction in righteousness."*

Uncle. Therefore you must not read the Scriptures as you read other books, but with great reverence and sacred awe. It is a message from God. If God should send you a message from heaven by the hand of any man, would you not receive it with great solemnity?

Hilary. I think I should tremble with fear.

Uncle. No doubt; and such should be our awe in approaching the Scriptures. They are messages from heaven. If Jesus Christ should write you a letter, with his own hand, how would you feel when you received it?

Ernest. We should be almost afraid to open it; but we should also be very desirous to know what it contained.

Uncle. Yes, and you would read it again and again : you would preserve it with the greatest care : and you would believe every word of it. So

---

* 2 Tim. iii. 16.

also, if you were invited to go to a certain place where you might hear God speaking to you from heaven, you would lay aside every careless thought, and listen with profound attention. Now we do really hear God speaking to us in the Holy Scriptures. Keep this always in mind. This direction is the most important of all I have to give you; indeed, it is the foundation of all the rest. Whenever you take this blessed volume into your hands, say to yourselves: "This is God's book: *I will hear what God the Lord will speak.*"*

Ernest. That reminds me of what I have read in the History of England, about that pious young king, Edward the Sixth. He was once playing with some of his companions, and wished to take down something from a shelf above his reach. One of his playfellows offered him a large book to stand upon; but when King Edward perceived it to be a Bible, he refused to use it in that way; and said, it was not proper that he should trample under his feet that which he ought to treasure up in his head and heart.

Uncle. This was very well said. Let us be careful, however, to reverence not the mere *outside* of the book, but its inspired contents. I will now proceed.

---

* Psalm lxxxv. 8.

Direction II.

PRAY FOR DIVINE AID AND ILLUMINATION.

The Bible contains many things which are mysterious, and which we could never have found out for ourselves. We need the assistance of God's Holy Spirit to make these things plain to us. Our sins darken our minds, so that we are liable to make mistakes in religious things ; and some of these mistakes are so great that they may even ruin the soul. David often prays for this divine illumination ; especially in the longest psalm in the Bible. Can either of you tell me which that is ?

Hilary. It is the hundred and ninteenth.

Uncle. True. David there prays : " Open thou mine eyes, that I may behold wondrous things out of thy law." And this is a suitable petition for us, whenever we open the Bible. Again, " Make me to understand thy precepts : so shall I talk of thy wondrous works." " Teach me, O Lord, the way of thy statutes ; and I shall keep it unto the end."

Without the assistance of God we cannot comprehend spiritual things. Thus it is said : " The natural man receiveth not the things of the Spirit of God ; for they are foolishness unto him : neither

can he know them, because they are spiritually dis-
cerned."*

Pray, my dear children, that the Lord would
take away this darkness of your minds. The
teaching of the Holy Spirit will do more to explain
to you the meaning of the Scriptures, than the best
human teachers. In this way some very poor men,
who were ignorant of human science, have become
wonderfully instructed in the things of God.

Ernest. Do you mean that we ought to pray
every time we are going to read in the Bible?

Uncle. I do not mean that you should actually
go down upon your knees, every time you begin
to read; although there would be nothing wrong
in this. But whenever you open the Scriptures,
it would be well for you to lift up your heart to
God in prayer, that he would enlighten your
mind. This you should likewise frequently do in
the midst of your reading; and when you close the
book, you should, in the same manner, beg that the
Holy Spirit would impress on your heart what you
have learned.

Direction III.

READ WITH PATIENCE AND SELF-DENIAL.

Ernest. What do you mean by reading with
patience?

---

* 1 Cor. ii. 14.

Uncle. By this I mean that you should not allow yourself to grow weary, so as to hurry over what you read, or lay the book aside. This is an important rule, particularly for youth; who are willing enough to read for a little while, but are glad to close the volume, and turn to something else. Besides this, you may observe that some young persons begin to study the Scriptures, and continue to do so regularly for a few weeks or months; but at the end of a short period their perseverance fails, and they neglect it altogether. You must not grow weary of the word of God. You must not read by fits and starts. You must not allow any thing to draw you away from the habit of constantly studying it.

Ernest. What do you mean by reading with *self-denial.*

Uncle. Self-denial means going against our own wishes for the sake of duty. To deny ourselves is to do what is not agreeable to us, when we are convinced that it is our duty; or to keep from enjoying any thing which we may like, when we are convinced that it would be wrong. Sometimes it may be the case, that when the time comes which you have set for reading the Scriptures, you may be in company, or at play, or reading some other book. Now you must exercise self-denial by giving up these worldly enjoyments for the sake of the Scriptures. Or, while you are actually reading, you may be tempted to leave off, for some other employment, or for some amusement. Here you must exercise self-denial, by persevering in the study of the Scriptures.

Hilary. But what are we to do, if we become very weary or sleepy ? Must we read on ?

Uncle. I think not. What we do under great weariness or drowsiness is not usually very profitable. In such a case, I should advise you to lay the book aside; always taking care, however, to make up what you have thus lost, at the earliest opportunity.

Direction IV.

READ THE SCRIPTURES WITH UNBROKEN ATTENTION.

Now do you understand this direction ?

Hilary. It means that we must not be thinking of other things while we read.

Uncle. Yes, this is part of what is meant. Some people fall into a habit of reading so carelessly, that they do not get a single idea from the words in the book. They read as if they were asleep. Make them close the book, and tell what the subject is, and they are absolutely dumb. The danger is greatest in books with which we are very familiar.

Did you never observe that when you have perused the same page a great many times, you have
caught yourselves repeating the words without
thinking of what they mean ?

Hilary. O yes, sir ! For when I commit a
speech to memory, to declaim it at school, I often
say it all over without once thinking what it is
about.

Ernest. And I have often taken notice, in repeating the Lord's prayer, that I go over the whole
while I am thinking of something else ; because I
am so familiar with the words.

Uncle. This is just the fault I wish you to avoid
in reading the Bible. *Read with attention.* Endeavour to think closely of every thing you read.
And besides this, let your attention be *unbroken.*
I have known a person to begin to read with great
seriousness ; but if he saw a bird near the window,
or heard the voice of a playmate, or even thought
of some favourite sport, his mind would be away
in a moment; his attention would be broken.
Guard against this wandering of thought. It is a
great evil in all study, but chiefly in the study of
the Scriptures.

Ernest. I acknowledge that I am guilty of this
fault every day ; but I hope I shall endeavour to
avoid it.

Direction V.

ENDEAVOUR TO LEARN SOMETHING NEW FROM EVERY VERSE BEFORE YOU LEAVE IT.

Hilary. Uncle, this seems to me to be a strange rule.

Uncle. How so, my child?

Hilary. Why, sir, if I really know what a verse means, how can I get any more from it?

Uncle. My dear boy, the Bible is a book very rich in meaning. I have read it over many, many times; and yet there is no passage in which, with proper attention, I cannot find something new. But you are to consider that we often read many verses together, without getting *any meaning whatever.* We have been so accustomed to the words of Scripture, having read them from our early childhood, that we feel satisfied to go over the language without learning any thing more about the sense.

I was led to lay down this rule for myself, from observing that I derived least profit from those parts of Scripture with which I was best acquainted. Thus, I often perused the Sermon on the Mount, with scarce a thought about its delightful contents. I therefore determined, that in my stated reading of the Scriptures, I would pause a little upon each verse, and not leave it until, if possible, I had learned from it something which did not strike me on the first perusal.

Ernest. But, uncle, it will take one a great while to get through the Bible, at this rate.

Uncle. Even if it should, it would be far more profitable than the ordinary way. But this direction applies only to the stated and regular study of the Scriptures; and I shall show you that sometimes it is desirable to read large portions together in a more rapid and cursory manner. Besides, you must know that thoughts move very quickly; we may have a number of thoughts in a second of time; and therefore the delay need not be so great as you suppose. There is moreover such a fulness of truth and meaning in the blessed Bible, that no man can ever say, in this world, of any one passage, that he has made himself master of all it teaches.

Ernest. Well, I begin to see more reason in the direction; and shall make trial of it.

Direction VI.

EXERCISE FAITH ON ALL THAT YOU READ.

Faith is belief. We have faith in that which we truly, and from the heart, believe. Ought we not to believe every word that is in the Bible?

Ernest. Yes, because every word is true. We should believe every word that God says.

Uncle. Remember the words of the apostle John, "If we receive the witness of men, the witness of God is greater."* It is not enough to hear or read the word of God; we must believe it. According to what the apostle Paul says of the ancient Israelites, "The word preached did not profit them, not being *mixed with faith* in them that heard it."†

There is no part of Scripture which can be properly read without faith. And this faith must be such as shall produce in us the very feelings intended by the divine Author in revealing the truth. Thus, when we read a command, faith will lead us to obey; when we read a threatening, to tremble; when we read a promise, to embrace it. Especially, when any thing is written concerning the blessed Saviour, faith will accept him, receive him, and lean upon him for salvation.

Often ask yourself, therefore, while you are reading, Do I really believe this from the heart? And often lift up your heart with the prayer of the apostles, "Lord, increase our faith!"

Direction VII.

READ WITH A WILLING AND OBEDIENT MIND.

Ernest. Have you not said something like this already?

---

* 1 John v. 9.　　　　　† Heb. iv. 2.

Uncle. I have, but I wish to call your attention more particularly to the duty of reading with an obedient disposition. The Bible teaches us chiefly two things, first, what we are to believe, and, secondly, what we are to do. The former calls for our faith, the latter for our obedience. Whatever God commands we are bound to do; and when we read any precept of the Scriptures, we should cherish the most cheerful and ready obedience. Without this, our reading will be of no use to us. This is what the apostle James teaches us: "Be ye *doers* of the word, and not hearers only."* This is what our Saviour also teaches in the parable of the sower. The good ground represents those hearers of the word who bring forth fruit, that is, yield obedience to the will of God. Indeed, our Lord seems to teach, that without this willing and obedient temper, no man can have an assured faith in the divine authority of what he learns : " If any man *will do his will,* he shall know of the doctrine, whether it be of God, or whether I speak of myself."† You will read the Scriptures with the greatest profit, when you are ready to say with little Samuel, " Speak, Lord, for thy servant heareth."‡

---

* James i. 22. † John vii. 17.

‡ 1 Sam. iii. 9.

Ernest. Dear uncle, does every one read the
Bible in this way ?

Uncle. Ah no ! I am sorry to say that many
read very carelessly ; and some who are very diligent in studying the word of God, learn it as a
mere task, just as they would learn any other lesson ; and seem never to think that it has any thing
to do with their own conduct. This leads me to
lay down another rule.

Direction VIII.

LET ALL THAT YOU READ BE APPLIED TO YOUR-
SELF IN THE WAY OF SELF-EXAMINATION.

Ernest. I am afraid I do not know what is meant
by applying what I read to myself.

Uncle. I will explain. Whenever you take up
your Bible, you should say within yourself, Now
I am going to read the message of God, and I must
endeavour to gain some improvement from it. So
you will be ready to turn every thing to some account
for the profit of your soul. Thus when you read the
history of any good man, you should try to copy
his excellences. When you read of any wicked
act, you should endeavour to avoid the like. When
you read of any Christian virtue or grace, you
should inquire whether you possess it, and seek to
attain it. Take, for instance, the Lord's prayer.
When you read *Forgive us our debts as we for-*

give our debtors; you should endeavour to offer up this prayer with a sincere heart, while you read. And in order to do this, you should ask yourself, whether you do from the heart forgive all those who have done you any evil; for unless you do thus forgive, you cannot truly offer this petition.* This is what I mean by *self-examination.*

By reading in this way, the best men who have ever lived have grown more and more holy. Every time they read a portion of Scripture, they are either convinced of some sin, and thus led to repentance; or awakened to the performance of some duty, and thus made more consistent Christians.

Direction IX.

SEEK TO HAVE YOUR AFFECTIONS STIRRED UP WHILE YOU READ.

Hilary. What do you mean by *affections?*

Uncle. I mean *feelings,* such as fear, joy, hope, desire, love, confidence, and the like.

Ernest. What do you mean by having these affections *stirred up?*

Uncle. I mean feeling in a lively manner, or having these affections warm and awakened. For instance, at some times when you are employed

---

* Matt. v. 44; vi. 12. Luke xi. 4.

about other things, you have scarcely any thoughts about your dear parents. But when you retuin home after an absence of some weeks, the sight of your father and mother will fill you with affection for them; perhaps your eyes will be filled with tears; your love will then be awakened. In other words, this affection will be stirred up. Does not the thought, even now, give you pleasure?

Hilary. O yes, sir! I long to see them very much.

Uncle. That is, you have a strong *desire* to see them; now the affection of *desire* is stirred up in your hearts. You also *hope* to see them before long; and this hope is another affection or feeling which is stirred up.

Most persons read the Scriptures without any warmth of feeling. They peruse God's message to them as coldly and insensibly as if it were a common book. This is what I wish you to avoid. When you read of God's anger against sin, you should be filled with godly *fear*. When you read of his goodness and mercy, you should be filled with *gratitude*. When you read of his glorious holiness, you should exercise *love*. And there is no part of the Bible in which there may not be found something to awaken some good feeling. Never allow yourself to read this blessed volume in a cold, unfeeling manner.

There is no method so proper for awakening devout feelings as the reading of the Holy Scriptures. For this reason, all pious persons have made this a part of their private devotions; and hence we are led to another important rule.

Direction X.

SET APART A SPECIAL TIME FOR DEVOTIONAL READING.

Ernest. Do you mean that we ought to have a certain hour of every day fixed for this purpose?

Uncle. Exactly. And by *devotional reading* I mean that reading which is intended not so much to communicate fresh knowledge as to warm our hearts. The proper time for this will be when you retire for private prayer.

Hilary. Is it best to have particular hours for secret prayer?

Uncle. I think it is. The holiest men have found it so. Otherwise we are apt to neglect the duty very often, or to omit it altogether. But if a certain hour be fixed, then whenever that hour comes, we shall be put in mind of the duty; and it will become habitual, so that we shall not be able to omit it without pain.

Ernest. What parts of the Bible are most proper at such times?

Uncle. Those parts which demand little explanation, being free from difficulty; and those parts which touch our feelings most sensibly. Thus the Psalms of David, and the history and discourses of our Saviour in the gospels, will be found exceedingly profitable. I would advise you, when you go to your private room or closet for prayer, to begin by lifting up your heart to God for a moment or two, to ask his blessing. Then take the Bible, and turn to some passage of the kind I have mentioned. A very few verses will, in most cases, be sufficient. Read these with the greatest attention and reverence. You need not perplex yourself with difficulties, nor dwell even upon those questions which might be very proper at another time. But endeavour to have your heart affected with the excellency of divine things. After this it will be proper for you to engage in your solemn prayers. And I hope, my dear children, that by the grace of God, you will be enabled to say, that these are the happiest hours of your whole life. Let us now go on to the next in order.

Direction XI.

KEEP THE LORD JESUS IN VIEW IN ALL YOU READ.

Ernest. But is there not a great deal in the Bible which does not relate to Christ?

Uncle. The Bible contains many passages which do not teach any thing *directly* concerning Christ.

But, at the same time, Christ is the great subject of the whole Scriptures. Both Testaments testify of him. Thus he said to the Jews, " Search the Scriptures," (or as some read it, " Ye do search the Scriptures,") " they are they which testify of me."* The Old Testament prepared the way for the Messiah, the New Testament reveals him. The history of the Old Testament is chiefly a history of Christ's progenitors. The rites and ceremonies of the Jewish worship were filled with types or emblems of Christ. The prophecies predict his coming and his work; and the New Testament is entirely taken up with what relates to him.

The great use of the Bible is to make us acquainted with the Redeemer. " This is life eternal; that they might know Thee, the only true God, and Jesus Christ whom thou hast sent."† We should therefore seek this knowledge in every part of the Scriptures. " To *him*," says the apostle Peter, " give all the prophets witness, that through his name whosoever believeth in him shall receive remission of sins."‡

I will here read you a short extract from the works of the excellent Leighton: " Let this also commend the Scriptures much to our diligence and

---

* John v. 39.   † John xvii. 3   ‡ Acts x. 43.

affection, that their great theme is our Redeemer, and salvation wrought by him ; that they contain the display of his excellencies, and are the lively picture of his matchless beauty. Were we more engaged in reading them, we should daily see more of him in them, and so of necessity love him more."

The great question for every one of us is, *What must I do to be saved?* The Bible answers this question by showing us the Lord Jesus Christ, as our divine Redeemer. Therefore keep him always in view while you read.

Ernest. Every word you say, my dear uncle, makes me feel condemned for having paid so little attention to this best of books.

Uncle. The feeling is natural and reasonable ; and the last direction which I shall give you this evening is this :

Direction XII.

Read the Bible more than any thing else.

Hilary. But how can we do this, when we have so many hundred other books to read ?

Uncle. This is the book of books—the best of all—worth all the rest put together. If all other books were destroyed, you might still be led to eternal salvation by this alone.

Other books are to be read at proper times, and

occasionally ; but the Bible is to be read every day
There are many thousands of books in the world,
and we have so many within our reach, that we are
often tempted to neglect the Scriptures. But all
the learning of all the wise men that ever lived is
not to be compared with the wisdom of this book.
If the Bible were more constantly read, the earth
would be filled with better Christians.

Hilary. Is there no danger of becoming weary
of reading so much in one book ?

Uncle. Those who read the Bible most, love it
best. They find something new in it at every
fresh perusal. They prefer it to all other books,
and can say with David, " O how I love thy law !
It is my meditation all the day."

Let me here relate an anecdote of the celebrated
Dr. Buchanan. Shortly before his death this good
man was talking to some of his friends about the
great pains he had taken to have the Syriac New
Testament correctly printed. He mentioned that
he read over every page *five times*, before it
went to the press. He said, he had expected
beforehand that this would have been tiresome,
but that every fresh perusal of the sacred page
seemed to unveil new beauties. Here he stop
ped, and burst into tears. " Do not be alarmed,"
said he, as soon as he had recovered himself, " I
could not suppress the emotion I felt as I recollected

the delight it pleased God to afford me in the read
ing of his word."

I have also read a pleasing account of a conversation between Count Oxenstiern, Chancellor of
Sweden, and Whitlock, an English ambassador.
The count, who was one of the greatest men of his
age, was at this time living in retirement. "I have
seen much," said he, "and enjoyed much of this
world, but I never knew how to live till now. I
thank my good God, who has given me time to
know him, and also myself. All the comfort I
have, and which is more than the whole world can
give, is the knowledge of God's love in my heart,
and *the reading of this blessed book;*" and here he
laid his hand on the Bible.

Hilary. I remember, uncle, that you told us in
the first conversation after we came, that the Bible
was the most interesting book in the world.

Uncle. Yes ; and this has been the opinion of
the greatest men. Sir William Jones, who was
acquainted with many languages, and was one of
the most learned and accomplished scholars who
ever lived, wrote the following words in the blank
leaf of his Bible :

" I have regularly and attentively perused these
Holy Scriptures, and am of opinion, that this volume, independently of its divine origin, contains
more true sublimity, more exquisite beauty, more

pure morality, more important history, and finer strains of poetry and eloquence, than can be collected from all other books, in whatever age or language they may have been written." Let me, therefore, exhort you, my dear nephews, to devote yourselves to the study of the Scriptures. But the evening is passing away, and I will reserve what I have still to say, until to-morrow and the day after.

CHAPTER XVII.

Rules for the reading of Scripture, continued :—The Bible must be read daily—In regular course—Neglecting no part—In suitable portions—Without prejudice—Comparing scriptu.e with scripture—With judicious use of commentaries, and abundant perusal of the text itself—The Bible our study for life.

As the time for their departure drew nigh, the boys became more and more anxious to receive all the instructions which their uncle had to communicate. At an early hour, the next evening, they reminded him that he had promised to continue his directions for reading the Scriptures ; and their good uncle, with a benignant countenance, began as follows.

Uncle. I have already given you twelve directions ; I shall now proceed to give you about as many more.

Direction XIII.

READ THE BIBLE DAILY.

There was a celebrated Greek painter, who accomplished such a number of works as surprised his friends, until he told them that his motto was, *No day without a line.* A little every day will effect a great deal in the course of a year. It is constant dropping which wears away the rocks. Hence it is far more important to read a portion every day, even though it be only a few verses, than to read many chapters at once, but at irregular intervals. The Holy Scriptures are the nourishment of our souls, just as food is of our bodies ; and we should be as unwilling to omit our daily portion of the word of God, as to miss one of our ordinary meals.

Ernest. Some people read the Bible only on Sundays.

Uncle. The Lord's-day is a very suitable time for reading the Scriptures; indeed, this should be one our chief employments on that day. But we need the light of God's truth every day that we live. The psalmist calls the Scriptures the *man of his counsel;* that is, his adviser. We should seek the advice and counsel of God day by day. It is a good thing to keep our minds constantly under the influence of divine truth. This has been the practice of good men, even of those who have had many laborious occupations to distract their attention. I suppose you have both read Miss Hannah More's beautiful tract, called "The Shepherd of Salisbury Plain."

Hilary. Yes, sir ; we have read it a number of times ; and we have also read in other books about this shepherd.

Ernest. It is all a true story, and his real name was David Saunders.

Uncle. Very well. Now what I was about to tell you is this. David Saunders once said to Dr. Stonehouse :—"Blessed be God! through his mercy I learned to read when I was a boy. I believe there is no day, for the last thirty years, that I have not peeped at my Bible. If we can't find time to read a chapter, I defy any man to say he can't find time to read a verse; and a single verse, well followed and put in practice every day, would make no bad figure at the year's end; three hundred and sixty-five texts, without the loss of a moment's time, would make a pretty stock, a little golden treasury, as one may say, from new-year's day to new-year's day; and if children were brought up to it, they would come to look for their text as naturally as they do for their breakfast. I can say the greatest part of my Bible by heart. I have led but a lonely life, and have often had but little to eat; but my Bible has been meat, drink, and company to me; and when want and trouble have come upon me, I don't know what I should have done indeed, if I had not had the promises of this book for my stay and support."

Ernest. That is a beautiful anecdote; it is one of the things which I will try to remember.

Uncle. I have said enough on this head.

Direction XIV.

READ IN REGULAR COURSE.

Ernest. Do you mean that we should begin at Genesis and read through to Revelation?

Uncle. I do; and when you have gone through once, begin again, and re-peruse the whole, and so continue during the remainder of your life.

Hilary. But should we never read in any other place?

Uncle. I do not mean that. I have already advised you to make selections for your devotional reading. Likewise, at other times, you may turn over the pages of your Bible, and pick out such places as suit your present state of mind. But still, there should be some hour of the day in which you should be regularly and systematically going through the whole revelation of God.

Ernest. But according to this, we might be for many months reading the Old Testament, without looking at the New; or reading the New Testament without looking at the Old.

Uncle. I have thought of this; and to prevent this evil, I recommend to you a method which I have pursued myself; which is, to read daily in both Testaments; a portion of one in the morning, and a portion of the other in the evening. Or, what is the same thing, read each Testament separately, over and over, in course.

Hilary. What advantage is there in this regular method?

Uncle. It has many advantages. In this way you always complete one book before you begin another. Thus you are able to observe the connexion of the parts. You also get every part of the instruction just in its proper place. And you are moreover secured against the evil of omitting any portion. But this is so important, that you may write it down by itself.

Direction XV.

Neglect no part of Scripture.

Those who read the Bible at random can scarcely avoid this. Even after several years' study, there will be passages to which they have paid no special attention.

Ernest. But are not some parts of Scripture more important than others?

Uncle. Certainly. But unless we read *every* part, we shall not be likely to find out which these important parts are. Having once discovered this, we may read them over and over, at other times, as often as we choose. But " *all Scripture* is given by inspiration of God, and is profitable for doctrine, for reproof, for correction, for instruction in righteousness."*

We do not always know while we are reading, what portions will prove most useful to us. I have often found myself warned, instructed, and comforted, by the recollection of texts which appeared to me very unimportant while I was perusing them. Therefore we ought to neglect no portion of Scripture.

Hilary. I have always read most in the New Testament.

Uncle. This is usually the case. Many persons go through life altogether ignorant of the delightful histories and glorious prophecies of the Old Testament. You will be careful to avoid this error, and the observance of the preceding rule will be of the greatest advantage to you.

Direction XVI.

LET YOUR DAILY PORTION BE OF PROPER LENGTH; NEITHER TOO MUCH NOR TOO LITTLE

Ernest. How much is a proper quantity?

Uncle. That is a question which every one must answer for himself. Some men have more leisure than others ; some grow weary of their book much sooner than others. The learned Dr. Gouge used

---

* 2 Tim. iii. 16.

to read fifteen chapters daily; and I suppose the good shepherd of Salisbury plain, on his busy days, read only as many verses.

Ernest. But is it not best to have a fixed portion for every day?

Uncle. I think it is. On the Lord's-day one can, of course, read more than on other days. There are many good methods of dividing the Scriptures so as to read them through once every year. I have found the following division very convenient.

Five chapters every Sunday, and three chapters on each of the other days, will take you through the Bible in a year.

The next rule which I have to give you will be of more value to you when you are older; but you may write it down, and learn the meaning of it. It is this:

Direction XVII.

READ FOR YOURSELF; IMPARTIALLY, AND WITHOUT PREJUDICE.

That is, do not cling to your preconceived opinions, when the Bible is against them.

Ernest. What are preconceived opinions?

Uncle. When any one makes up his mind upon any point, before he examines what the Bible teaches, this opinion of his is a preconceived opinion; and very often it is altogether wrong. For example, I have a neighbour who is a Universalist; that is, he does not believe in any future punishment. He formed this opinion without looking at the Scripture, and now he is so full of prejudice that he cannot read with impartiality. He is unable to see that the whole Bible is against him. The right way is to get all our doctrines from the Scriptures. We never can be secure in believing any thing unless we find it there revealed.

Ernest. Ought we not to believe every thing which is preached by ministers of the gospel?

Uncle. Not at all; we are to believe them just so far as they agree with the word of God. At the same time, we should always listen to their words with an humble, teachable mind. It is very dangerous to indulge a spirit of criticism, contradiction, and perpetual doubt. Yet you remember what is said of those Bereans who heard the preaching of Saul and Silas: "These were more noble than those in Thessalonica, in that they received the word with all readiness of mind, and *searched the Scriptures daily, whether these things were so.*"*

Hilary. I have heard that the Catholics are not allowed to do this.

Uncle. They are not. This is one grand differ-

* Acts xvii. 11.

ence between Protestants and Papists. The Protestant claims the right of judging for himself; the Papist is bound to believe just what the church says.

Direction XVIII.

IN EVERY PASSAGE, TRY TO HAVE BEFORE YOUR MIND THE WHOLE SCENE, AND ALL THE CIRCUMSTANCES.

Ernest. Please to make this rule plainer.

Uncle. In plainer language: whenever you read any account in the Scriptures, *try to feel as if you were there.* Bring up before your mind all the circumstances. Consider who is the *writer* or *speaker;* observe *to whom* the words were addressed. If it is an historical transaction, learn all you can about the *time*, the *place*, the surrounding objects, and the persons present. In order to do this, you will find it useful to be familiar with biblical geography, manners, and customs.

Hilary. Perhaps, sir, you can make this more clear by an example.

Uncle. I will endeavour to do so. In the nineteenth and twentieth chapters of Exodus, we have a sublime description of the giving of the law. But a mere hasty perusal of these chapters will not make a sufficient impression on your minds. You must try to bring it up before your view, as if you had actually beheld it. Consider the *time:* it was nearly fifteen hundred years before Christ. Consider the *place:* it was Mount Sinai in Arabia. And here you must try to find out every thing about this mountain and desert, by means of maps, plates, and descriptions. Consider the *persons:* here were more than a million of Israelites, encamped around this mountain. Then try to get a distinct idea of the scene. The vast multitudes are trembling with awful expectation. The mountain is wrapt in clouds and fire; there are thunders and lightnings, and the sound of a dreadful mysterious trumpet. The smoke of Sinai ascends, as if it were a mighty furnace. Moses and Aaron approach, and hear the voice of Jehovah. Now, if you can have all these circumstances before your mind, the effect will be great and lasting.

So also, in every other part of the Bible, you must, as far as possible, place yourself in the very midst of the scene which is represented.

Hilary. This rule is very new to me; but I perceive that it will assist us very much in understanding what we read.

Direction XIX.
COMPARE PASSAGE WITH PASSAGE.

Ernest. I think, sir, you have once before advised us to do this, when you were speaking of the marginal references.

Uncle. I did so. And therefore I need only

now remind you of what I then said, particularly of the remarks of Bishop Horsley, which I read to you.* Let me, however, add to these the observations of the pious Dr. Scott. This learned man made a very laborious collection of marginal references, amounting in number to many thousands. He was therefore well qualified to judge what would be the effects of this method of studying Scripture. Now hear what he says : " Though I had for many years previously studied the Scriptures as my one grand business, I can truly aver that the insight which I have thus obtained into many parts, which before I had not so carefully noted, is so great, as abundantly to repay my labour, and to convince me, that, along with other means, consulting well-selected marginal references forms one of the best helps for fixing the word of God in the memory, leading the mind to a just interpretation of it, and in many cases rendering it most affecting to the heart.—To those who desire to study the Scriptures accurately and deeply, I would very earnestly recommend to set apart an hour, or half an hour, every day, when it can be done ; and regularly to go through the Scriptures, carefully consulting all the references."†

---

* See pp. 155, 156.

† The language of the quotation has been somewhat simplified.

Direction XX.

PAY SPECIAL ATTENTION TO THE CONNEXION
AND SCOPE OF EVERY PASSAGE.

By the *connexion*, I mean what goes before and
after the passage. By the *scope*, I mean the inten-
tion of the writer, or what he is aiming to prove or
teach. In other words, always bear in mind what
the sacred penman is writing about.

Many readers altogether neglect the connexion
of passages. They read perhaps a single chapter
at a time, without looking back to see what the
preceding chapter was about, or looking forward to
see what comes next. Now it is impossible to get
the full meaning of any book, by reading it in this
way. The direction I have just given is particularly important in several of the epistles ; where
there is a great deal of reasoning or argument.

Again, we must always consider the *scope* of a
passage ; that is, what it is intended to teach ; or
we shall fall into very great mistakes. Thus many
of our Lord's beautiful parables have been misun-
derstood and grossly perverted.

Direction XXI.

MAKE A JUDICIOUS USE OF COMMENTARIES.

Ernest. I have heard Mr. Derby say that he
never needs any commentary.

Uncle. Mr. Derby must be a very wise man indeed. For my part, I find some need of a good commentary almost every day.

Hilary. But some of the commentaries are so very large, and in so many great volumes, that I should think it would take half a lifetime to read them through.

Uncle. I would by no means advise you to read a large commentary *through*. For this reason, I have recommended a *judicious* use of these helps. By reading too much of a commentary, we shall be led to read too little of the text. The use of a commentary is to explain to us that which it is difficult to understand. Where a passage is perfectly plain, or has been already explained to us, it is often a loss of time to read any explanation of it. But there are many real difficulties in the Bible, and here we need the help of those wise and good men who have spent their lives in the study of the Scriptures.

Hilary. What commentary would you recommend to us?

Uncle. There are so many that are excellent, that I shall not undertake to choose for you. On this point, you had better take the advice of your minister. Always bear in mind, however, that the text, rather than any explanation of it, should be your great study. For this reason, I add:

Direction XXII.

READ THE TEXT ABUNDANTLY.

By the *text*, I here mean the very words of the Scripture. This should be our great study. Some persons read some five or six verses of the text, and then spend an hour or more in reading notes upon it. Just the reverse of this seems to me to be the proper method. I have always observed that those who read most largely in the text of Scripture, are most acquainted with its meaning. By continually reading over and over the same passages, and comparing one place with another, they have their greatest difficulties cleared up. One verse throws light upon another; and what is taught obscurely in one place, is expressed plainly and fully in another. Indeed, no man can well fail to be learned in the Scriptures, who goes on from day to day, reading large portions, in regular order, and with devout attention.

Hilary. Might there not be danger of one's running on too fast?

Uncle. Certainly. You should have your set times, for not only reading, but *studying* the Scriptures. At these times, let no difficulty pass without an attempt to have it explained. But you should often, at other times, take up the Bible, for the express purpose of rapid and cursory reading;

just as you would peruse any other very interesting volume. At such times, you may read a number of chapters at one sitting. I have found the greatest profit and pleasure in thus going over a whole book or epistle in the course of one day. This brings the whole subject before the mind at one view ; and if you will persevere in sometimes reading the same book over and over a number of times before you leave it, you will find it delightful and more clear at each repetition.

Ernest. Dear uncle, you talk as if we had a great deal of time upon our hands ; and as if we had nothing else to do but to read the Bible.

Uncle. I will reply to you by another rule :

Direction XXIII.

REMEMBER THAT THIS BOOK IS TO BE THE STUDY OF YOUR WHOLE LIFE.

This must be your one book, more loved and more studied than all others. If I were to take down one of my great folio volumes, and say, ' Boys, you must take this book, and read it over twenty times;' you might very properly answer: ' Life is too short, for we have many other books to read.' But when I say this of the Bible, there is no propriety in such a reply. For the Bible is given to us to be our instructer and counsellor as long as we live. Be patient and persevering, and consider that this is a study which you are never to leave off, as long as you live. Although I have advised you to a course of scriptural study, which may seem to require a great deal of time, you are not to suppose that the work is to be accomplished in a year, or even ten years, and then laid aside, as you lay aside your other studies. No; you will never see the day, in this world, in which you can say that you have now done with the Bible.

Hilary. And did those good men, whom you have spoken about, study the Bible in this way, as long as they lived ?

Uncle. Yes; and some of them even on their death-beds. Let me read you an account of the Venerable Bede, which is contained in this little volume.*

Ernest. Who was the person of whom you are about to read ?

Uncle. His name was Beda, or Bede, and he was an eminent servant of Christ, who lived in England more than a thousand years ago. He was called *Venerable* Bede, from the great dignity and holiness of his character. He translated the Bible into the Anglo-Saxon tongue, which was then the language of our forefathers.

---

* Anecdotes, published by the London Religious Tract Society.

One of his pupils gives the following narrative
of his last hours : " Many nights he passed without
sleep, yet rejoicing and giving thanks, unless when
a little slumber intervened. When he awoke, he
resumed his accustomed devotions, and, with ex-
panded hands, never ceased returning thanks to
God. In such solemn joy, we passed fifty days,
but during these days, besides the daily lectures
which he gave, he endeavoured to compose two
works, one of which was a translation of St. John's
gospel into English. It had been observed of him,
that he never knew what it was to do nothing ; and
after his breathing became still shorter, he dictated
cheerfully, and sometimes said, ' Make haste, I
know not how long I shall hold out ; my Maker
may take me away very soon.' On one occasion,
a pupil said to him, ' Most dear master, there is
yet one chapter wanting ; do you think it trouble-
some to be asked any more questions ?' He answered, ' It is no trouble ; take your pen, and write
fast.' He continued to converse cheerfully, and
while his friends wept as he told them they would
see him no more, they rejoiced to hear him say,
' It is now time for me to return to Him who made
me. The time of my dissolution draws near. I
desire to be dissolved and to be with Christ. Yes,
my soul desires to see Christ, my king, in his
beauty.' The pupil, before mentioned, said to

him, ' Dear master, one sentence is still wanting.'
He replied, ' Write quickly !' The young man
soon added, ' It is finished !' He answered, ' Thou
hast well said—all is finished ! Hold my head in
thy hands ; I shall delight to sit at the opposite
side of the room, on the holy spot at which I have
been accustomed to pray, and where, whilst sitting,
I can call upon my Father.' Being placed on the
floor of his little room, he sang, ' Glory be to the
Father, and to the Son, and to the Holy Ghost ;'
and expired as he uttered the last words." So
that this excellent man may be said to have died
while engaged in the study of the Holy Scriptures.

I shall now leave you for the evening ; and to-
morrow we will close our conversations with a few
additional rules.

CHAPTER XVIII.

Rules for the reading of Scripture, continued :—The Bible must
be read with ardent love—Charging memory with its instructions—The importance of self-examination, meditation, and
conversation on what has been read—Passages read should
be turned into prayer—This reading is for the salvation of the
soul—Recapitulation of rules—Conclusion.

THE last day of the visit to Oakdale had now
come, and when Ernest and Hilary entered the old
gentleman's study in the evening there was a sad-
ness in their countenances. Their aged friend had
been very kind to them, and had taught them many
useful things ; so that they were grieved at the
thought of leaving him. He perceived this, and
began his conversation with them in the following
words.

Uncle. My dear nephews, you are to leave my
house to-morrow, and perhaps we may never meet
again in this world. You see I am an old man,
and it would not be very strange if I should be
called out of this world before you ever revisit this
part of the country. I therefore try to give you
the best instructions which I can think of ; and I
hope they may be of use to you when I am dead
and gone.

Ernest. It makes us sorry, dear uncle, to hear you talk so. But I am sure both Hilary and I will endeavour to remember all your kind instructions.

Uncle. Let me then proceed with the rules.

Direction XXIV.

CHERISH ARDENT LOVE FOR THE SCRIPTURES.

I am persuaded that if I should write you any book of advice, you would feel great regard for it, out of love for *me.* But the Scriptures are given you by your heavenly Father; how much more should you honour and love them! Do you remember what David says about this?

Ernest. "O how I love thy law! It is my meditation all the day."*

Hilary. He also says, "I love thy commandments above gold; yea, above fine gold."†

Uncle. Very well repeated. He further says, "How sweet are thy words unto my taste! yea, sweeter than honey to my mouth."‡ This is the feeling of every pious soul: and the further we go in the knowledge of the Scriptures, the more shall we love them. Never allow yourselves to fall into the habit of reading them as a task, but open the

---

* Ps. cxix. 97. † Ps. cxix. 127.
‡ Ps. cxix. 103.

volume with constant delight. Cultivate this warmth of affection, and rebuke your own hearts when you find yourselves destitute of it.

I have read of a certain Mr. Harris, a tradesman of London, whose love for the Scripture was such, that when his eyesight became dim, he caused the book of Psalms, and almost all the New Testament, to be written with white ink on black paper, in letters an inch long; that he might still read the best of books in his old age.

Hilary. I have heard of persons who copied the Bible with their own hands.

Uncle. Yes, the emperor Theodosius is said to have done so with the New Testament. The reformer, Zuinglius, transcribed the Epistles of Paul, and committed them to memory. In the early period of the Reformation, when Bibles were very scarce, and when it was dangerous to possess them, there were many instances of this strong attachment. The poor persecuted Christians used to meet, for the reading of the Scriptures, in garrets and lofts, or on board vessels. In the reign of the popish king James II., when many good people feared the re-establishment of the Romish power, there was a pious man who copied out the whole Bible in short hand, for his own use, lest the Scriptures should be suppressed.

Direction XXV.

CHARGE YOUR MEMORY WITH ALL THAT YOU READ.

I suppose you need scarcely be told the reason for this direction.

Hilary. If we do not remember what we read, we might as well not read at all; it can do us no good.

Uncle. Very true; and in order to remember, we must *charge* our memory, as if we *told* memory to keep it safe. Do you always read in this way?

Ernest. Sometimes, I confess, what I read seems to slip out of my mind.

Uncle. This is, indeed, too commonly the case. With some people, *all* that they read slips out of their mind. When they have perused a certain portion, they shut the book, and never think of it again for that day. Ask them in the evening what they were reading about in the morning, and they cannot tell. This is sufficiently plain without any further explanation.

Ernest. I suppose you do not mean that we should try to get every verse 'by heart,' so as to be able to repeat it without book.

Uncle. Certainly not; but here is another rule, relating to this very point.

Direction XXVI.

COMMIT TO MEMORY SOME PORTION OF SCRIP-
TURE EVERY DAY.

There is great advantage in this practice. If
you have much of the Bible in your memory, you
will be able to think of these precious words when
you cannot have your book before you. This will
be very profitable, for it may serve to direct and
comfort you when you are travelling, or sick, or
during the hours of night. It will also help you to
understand those passages which you read.

Hilary. How much ought we to get each day ?

Uncle. You may begin with a single verse.
After a few weeks, you will find it so much easier,
that you will find no more difficulty in learning ten
or twelve verses, than you had at first in learning
one. The memory is greatly strengthened by
daily practice ; and this is another advantage which
your minds will receive from what I am recom-
mending. By degrees you will have many chapters, and even whole books of Scripture treasured
up in your memory.

Ernest. Are there any persons who know whole
books by memory ?

Uncle. There have been many such, as I shall
show you by several examples. The Reverend
Doctor Marryat began this practice in his early

youth, and pursued it so far, that he is said to have committed to memory the books of Job, Psalms, Proverbs, Ecclesiastes, Isaiah, all the lesser Prophets, and all the Epistles.

Hilary. I should think he would forget what he had learned.

Uncle. In order to prevent this, he used to repeat the whole, by memory, once every year. Here is another instance. Theodore Beza, a celebrated reformer, lived to such an age that he could not recollect things which he had heard a few minutes before. Yet at this very time, it is said that he was able to repeat the Epistles of Paul, which he had committed to memory when he was young.

Ernest. This really astonishes me; I did not know that such a thing was possible.

Uncle. Let it encourage you to make the attempt. Viscount Carteret, who was lord-lieutenant of Ireland, in 1724, could repeat from memory the whole of the New Testament. The same thing is said of Pierpont Edwards, son of President Edwards. But this is not all. The late Rev. Thomas Threlkeld, of Lancashire, in England, used to be called a *living concordance.* If any three words were mentioned, (unless they were such as occur in many passages,) he could immediately, without hesitation, assign the chapter and verse where they might be found ; or, if the chapter and verse were mentioned, he could repeat the words. I have heard the same thing related of the Rev. John Brown, of Haddington.

Ernest. Were these men of great genius and learning ?

Uncle. Most of them were so. But the same thing has been true of many unlearned and humble persons. One of the most remarkable instances of this was an old man of Stirling, in Scotland, who went by the name of Blind Alick. He had been blind from his childhood. He was sent to a common school to keep him out of mischief, and here he began to commit to memory what he heard the other scholars read. In other ways and places, he continued to seek the knowledge of the Scriptures ; and such was the success of this blind beggar, that he came at last to know the whole of the Bible, both Old and New Testaments, by heart.

His case excited the interest of many persons, and among others, of the late celebrated Professor Dugald Stewart. Alick was often examined, and the result was always satisfactory. You might repeat any passage of the Scripture, and he would tell you chapter and verse ; or you might tell him the chapter and verse, and he would repeat to you the passage, word for word. A gentleman, to puzzle him, read a verse of the Bible, with a slight alteration. Alick hesitated a moment, and then told him where it was to be found, but said it had not been correctly given; he then repeated it as it stood in the book. The gentleman then asked him for the ninetieth verse of the seventh chapter of Numbers. Alick was again puzzled for a moment, but quickly replied, "You are fooling me, sirs! there is no such verse—that chapter has only eighty-nine verses."

Ernest. How long ago did this happen?

Uncle. Blind Alick was still living in 1833, and I have never heard of his death. In relating to you these incidents, I do not suppose that either you or I could ever make such wonderful acquisitions. But at the same time, we should be encouraged to improve the talent which we actually possess. All of us might commit more of the Scriptures to memory than we do. And, as I have already said, even those parts which we do not commit to memory should be read with such care, that we may be able afterwards to recall them to our minds.

Direction XXVII.

EXAMINE YOURSELF ON WHAT YOU HAVE READ.

When you have read any chapter or chapters, and are about to close the book, it would be well to pause and ask yourself such questions as these:

What have I now been reading about? What persons have been mentioned? What doctrines have I learned from this passage? What precepts are here given, or what duty enforced? What example is here set before me? What is there in these verses which it may be important for me to recollect during the day?

Such questions will enable you to discover whether you have been attentive and faithful. If you find that you have passed over any thing negligently, you may return to the book, and make up the deficiency. In every case, this self-examination will fix in your memory what you have been reading. When you again take up the Bible, at your next stated hour for scriptural study, it will be proper to ask yourself similar questions about the passage last read. Thus you will always be sure to keep up the connexion of the parts.

Ernest. Might not two friends examine one another in this way?

Uncle. Yes; and where two read together, the exercise would be truly profitable. But even when pursued in the solitary manner which I have represented, it leads to great good. I find it a good method, when I have finished any book of Scripture, to recall to mind, as far as possible, all its contents. Also at night, I have often been profited by going over in my mind, as I have lain in bed, the Scripture passages which I had read during the day. This brings me to another important point.

Direction XXVIII.

MAKE WHAT YOU READ THE SUBJECT OF MEDITATION.

Here that sweet text of David may again be applied: " O how I love thy law ! *It is my meditation all the day.*"* No doubt this holy man turned the words of revelation in his thoughts, by day and by night. So should we do likewise. Thus God said to the Israelites : " These words, which I command thee this day, shall be in thy heart."† There is no better proof of our loving the word of God, than our having it constantly in our thoughts ; and there is no happier method of keeping every thing evil out of our minds.

Dr. Doddridge, and other excellent writers, have recommended it as a useful practice, to select some text every morning, to be our special subject of meditation during the day. If we cannot do more, we can repeat to ourselves these sacred words, and thus exclude the vain imaginations which often vex us. This plan has been adopted by many of the best men I have ever known. It is but a few days

---

* Ps. cxix. 97. † Deut. vi. 6.

since I was reading the life of a very pious German bookseller, named Henry Julius Elers, who was an intimate friend and helper of the celebrated Francke.* The following statement is made concerning him. "Elers' preparation for every day consisted of a serious meditation on some important Scripture text, which he chose after his morning prayer. He received great benefit from this practice, and earnestly recommended it to others. He used to say, 'Such a text, deeply impressed on the heart, employs me all the day. I use it as a staff for my support. It secures me from distraction of mind during my business; and if I am called upon to instruct any one, I am never at a loss for a text.' He used to write down these daily texts in his memorandum book, and the last which he ever inserted in it was, 'Let your loins be girt about, and your lamps burning,' &c."†

Hilary. I think this is an excellent way. We might write down a text every day in a nice little book, and this would be worth preserving. And then we might commit these same texts to memory.

Uncle. Excellent, indeed! I hope you will both

---

* See Life of Francke, published by the American Sunday-school Union.

† Franken's Stiftungen, vol. ii. p. 466.

put it in practice ; as well as the other hints I have been giving you in our repeated conversations.

Ernest. Dear uncle, we have never heard so much conversation on these subjects before. What can be the reason that we scarcely ever hear people talking about the Bible ?

Uncle. It must arise from a want of interest in this blessed book, for " out of the abundance of the heart the mouth speaketh." But I have a special rule for this :

Direction XXIX.

FREQUENTLY CONVERSE ABOUT WHAT YOU HAVE BEEN READING.

Ernest. We often do so about other books which we read ; I frequently hear ladies and gentlemen talk an hour at a time about the last novel.

Uncle. That is because they love what they read. We should speak of the delightful truths of God's word. It will be natural to do so, if we have them much in our minds. But too often we read the Scriptures in a formal way, like a task, and seem glad to forget them when the book is closed. Observe that there is a special command in Scripture to do this very thing. " These words, which I command thee this day, shall be in thy heart. And thou shall teach them diligently unto thy children, and shall talk of them when thou sittest in thy house, and when thou walkest by the way, and when thou liest down, and when thou risest up."*

Hilary. But I should scarcely know how to begin to talk about the Bible.

Uncle. Just as you would about any other serious book in which you are interested. Not that you are to make set speeches, or speak beyond your knowledge. This would be vain and affected. But you may ask one another questions, or converse about Scripture characters; and as your knowledge increases, you will find a multitude of points relating to Scripture, upon which you may talk with your friends, to your great profit.

Direction XXX.

TURN WHAT YOU READ INTO PRAYER.

By observing this rule, you will find the Scriptures a perpetual help to your devotions. You will thus be taught, both how to pray, and what to pray for as you ought.

Ernest. Some passages in the Bible seem to me to be prayers already.

Uncle. That is very true; and in all such cases, the words may be profitably used, without alteration; provided that you repeat them with the spirit

---

* Deut. vi. 6, 7.

of prayer. Thus most passages in the Psalms of David are prayer; in which I include, not merely petition, but adoration, thanksgiving, and confession Thus, when David says, "Teach me to do thy will, for thou art my God!"* the words are a petition, and you should try to feel as David did, and earnestly offer the same prayer. Again, when he says, "I acknowledge my transgressions, and my sin is ever before me;"† you should endeavour to make this confession with real repentance of heart.

Ernest. But how can this be done in those other parts of Scripture which are not in the form of prayer?

Uncle. It is to such passages that the direction more particularly applies. These you must *turn into prayer.* For instance, if you read of a truly pious man, you may lift up your heart silently to God, in supplication for grace to enable you to follow the example. When you read a commandment, you may pray thus : "Lord, have mercy upon me, and incline my heart to keep this law." When you read a promise, you may pray that it may be fulfilled in yourself; thus, when God says, "My grace is sufficient for thee,"‡ you should pray, "O Lord, let thy grace ever be sufficient for *me!*" This rule agrees with one given by the

---

* Ps. cxliii. 10.   † Ps. li. 3.   ‡ 2 Cor. xii. 9.

Rev. Thomas Hartwell Horne, in his celebrated Introduction to the Study of Scripture: he says, " The words of the passage selected for our private reading, after its import has been ascertained, may beneficially be summed up, or comprised in very brief prayers or ejaculations."

Hilary. What is the meaning of *ejaculations ?*

Uncle. It is derived from a Latin word which means to *throw a dart.* Ejaculations are short prayers, offered during other employments, and, as it were, *darted forth towards heaven.* This direction applies most to your private reading for devotional purposes.

And now I have come to the very last of my rules. And I beg you, my beloved nephews, to bear in your minds what I am now about to say to you.

Direction XXXI.

IN ALL YOUR READING, REMEMBER THAT IT IS FOR THE SALVATION OF YOUR SOUL.

This, my dear boys, is the reason why I have been so earnest in exhorting you to the study of the Bible. All your other studies and attainments extend their influence only to this life; here is a book which makes wise unto salvation. Many of the most learned men in the world have had no spiritual knowledge of the Lord Jesus Christ; and therefore their souls have perished. Dreadful thought! For of what advantage can all human learning be to any man, if at last he goes away into everlasting fire! Remember the words of the Lord Jesus, *What shall it profit a man, if he shall gain the whole world, and lose his own soul?** I am, therefore, unspeakably anxious about you, lest you should neglect this great salvation.

Young persons are too apt to forget the importance of these things. You feel strong and cheerful now, and expect a long life of many pleasures. But consider, that in a single day, yes, a single moment, you may be brought to death. The greater part of the human race never reach the age of manhood. And even if your lives should be spared, how many things may happen to lead you astray, and ruin your immortal soul. I perceive that these things now affect you; I am glad that they do so. But if you allow these youthful impressions to wear away, you will probably become more hardened and impenitent, the older you grow. Hear the word of God, saying to you, " Remember *now* thy Creator, in the days of thy youth."† Many persons are now in perdition, who were instructed in religion, and who felt just as you now

---

* Mark viii. 36.　　　　　† Eccl. xii. 1.

do, when they were young; but they resisted the
Holy Spirit, and died in their sins. I pray that
this may never be the case with you.

Whenever you open the Scriptures, let this
thought be in your minds; and pray that God
would bless all that you read, to the salvation of
your souls. Do not think, however, that the mere
knowledge of what is in the Bible will secure this
blessing. Many have been diligent students of the
Scriptures, who have never felt its saving effects.
A man may know the whole Bible by memory, and
yet be destitute of true religion. Hence it is of the
utmost importance that you should read with the
right spirit, and especially that you should have the
blessing of God upon what you read.

We are now about to separate. Before many
days, I must depart from this world; but I hope,
when we all stand before our Judge, we shall meet
with joy, and hear from his lips those gracious
words : " Come, ye blessed of my Father, inherit
the kingdom prepared for you from the foundation
of the world."*

That this may be our blessed lot, let us now
pray to God.

Here the boys, who were affected even to tears

---

* Matt. xxv. 34.

knelt down, and their uncle offered up an earnest and affectionate prayer for them.

After this he requested them to read over the directions he had given them; which were as follows:

DIRECTIONS FOR READING THE BIBLE.

I. In all your reading of the Bible, bear in mind that it is the word of God.

II. Pray for divine aid and illumination.

III. Read with patience and self-denial.

IV. Read with unbroken attention.

V. Endeavour to learn something new from every verse, before you leave it.

VI. Exercise faith on all that you read.

VII. Read with a willing and obedient mind.

VIII. Let all that you read be applied to yourselves, in the way of self-examination.

IX. Seek to have your affections stirred up while you read.

X. Set apart a special time for devotional reading.

XI. Keep the Lord Jesus in view, in all that you read.

XII. Read the Bible more than any thing else.

XIII. Read the Bible daily.

XIV. Read in regular course.

XV. Neglect no part of Scripture.

XVI. Let your daily portion be of proper length ; neither too much nor too little.

XVII. Read for yourself ; impartially, and without prejudice.

XVIII. In every passage, try to have before your mind the whole scene, and all the circumstances.

XIX. Compare passage with passage.

XX. Pay special attention to the connexion and scope of every passage.

XXI. Make a judicious use of commentaries.

XXII. Read the text abundantly.

XXIII. Remember that this book is to be the study of your life.

XXIV. Cherish ardent love for the Scriptures.

XXV. Charge your memory with all that you read.

XXVI. Commit to memory some portion of Scripture every day.

XXVII. Examine yourself on what you have read.

XXVIII. Make what you have read the subject of meditation.

XXIX. Frequently converse about what you have been reading.

XXX. Turn what you read into prayer.

XXXI. In all your reading, remember that it is for the salvation of your soul.

Here they parted with their dear old uncle for the night; and the next morning, at an early hour, their father's carriage arrived, and they returned to New York.

THE END.

Other SGCB Classic Reprints

In addition to *The Scripture Guide* which you now hold in your hands, Solid Ground Christian Books is honored to present the following titles, many for the first time in more than a century:

THEOLOGY ON FIRE: *Sermons from the Heart of J.A. Alexander*
A SHEPHERD'S HEART: *Sermons from the Ministry of J.W. Alexander*
EVANGELICAL TRUTH: *Sermons for the Christian Home by A. Alexander*
CALVINISM IN HISTORY *by Nathaniel S. McFetridge*
OPENING SCRIPTURE: *A Hermeneutical Manual by Patrick Fairbairn*
THE ASSURANCE OF FAITH *by Louis Berkhof*
THE PASTOR IN THE SICK ROOM *by John D. Wells*
THE BUNYAN OF BROOKLYN: *The Life & Sermons of Ichabod Spencer*
THE NATIONAL PREACHER: *Sermons from the 2nd Great Awakening*
THE POOR MAN'S OT COMMENTARY *by Robert Hawker (6 vols)*
THE POOR MAN'S NT COMMENTARY *by Robert Hawker (3 vols)*
FIRST THINGS: *The First Lessons God Taught Mankind by Gardiner Spring*
BIBLICAL & THEOLOGICAL STUDIES *by the 1912 Faculty of Princeton*
THE POWER OF GOD UNTO SALVATION *by B.B. Warfield*
THE LORD OF GLORY *by B.B. Warfield*
A GENTLEMAN & A SCHOLAR: *Memoir of J.P. Boyce by John Broadus*
SERMONS TO THE NATURAL MAN *by W.G.T. Shedd*
SERMONS TO THE SPIRITUAL MAN *by W.G.T. Shedd*
HOMILETICS AND PASTORAL THEOLOGY *by W.G.T. Shedd*
A PASTOR'S SKETCHES 1 & 2 *by Ichabod S. Spencer*
THE PREACHER AND HIS MODELS *by James Stalker*
IMAGO CHRISTI *by James Stalker*
A HISTORY OF PREACHING *by Edwin C. Dargan*
LECTURES ON THE HISTORY OF PREACHING *by John A. Broadus*
THE SCOTTISH PULPIT *by William Taylor*
THE SHORTER CATECHISM ILLUSTRATED *by John Whitecross*
THE CHURCH MEMBER'S GUIDE *by John Angell James*
THE SUNDAY SCHOOL TEACHER'S GUIDE *by John Angell James*
CHRIST IN SONG: *Hymns of Immanuel from All Ages by Philip Schaff*
COME YE APART: *Daily Words from the Four Gospels by J.R. Miller*
DEVOTIONAL LIFE OF THE S.S. TEACHER *by J.R. Miller*

Call us Toll Free at 1-877-666-9469
Send us an e-mail at sgcb@charter.net
Visit us on line at solid-ground-books.com

Uncovering Buried Treasure to the Glory of God

Printed in the United States
144492LV00003B/29/A